3G Marketing on the Internet

Seventh Edition

Third Generation Internet Marketing Strategies for Online Success

Susan Sweeney

Andy MacLellan

Ed Dorey

MAXIMUM PRESS
605 Silverthorn Road
Gulf Breeze, FL 32561
(850) 934-0819
www.maxpress.com

Publisher: Jim Hoskins

Manager of Finance/Administration: Joyce Reedy

Production Manager: Gina Cooke

Cover Designer: Lauren Smith

Copyeditor: Ellen Falk

Proofreader: Kathy Lord

Indexer: Susan Olason

Printer: P.A. Hutchison

This publication is designed to provide accurate and authoritative information in regard to the subject matter covered. It is sold with the understanding that the publisher is not engaged in rendering professional services. If legal, accounting, medical, psychological, or any other expert assistance is required, the services of a competent professional person should be sought. ADAPTED FROM A DECLARATION OF PRINCIPLES OF A JOINT COMMITTEE OF THE AMERICAN BAR ASSOCIATION AND PUBLISHERS.

Library of Congress Cataloging-in-Publication Data

Sweeney, Susan, 1956-
3G marketing on the internet : third generation internet marketing strategies for online success / Susan Sweeney, Ed Dorey & Andy MacLellan.— 7th ed.
p. cm.
Includes index.
ISBN 1-931644-37-3 (pbk.)
1. Internet marketing. 2. Internet advertising. 3. Electronic commerce. I. Title: Three G marketing on the internet. II. Dorey, Ed, 1976- III. MacLellan, Andy, 1979- IV. Title.
HF5415.1265.S92 2006
658.8'72—dc22
2005033908

3G Marketing on the Internet

Other Titles of Interest From Maximum Press

More *IBM-Related* Books

- *Building an On Demand Computing Environment with IBM*

- *IBM Software for e-business on demand*

- *Exploring IBM @server pSeries*

- *Exploring IBM @server iSeries*

- *Exploring IBM @server xSeries*

- *Exploring IBM @server zSeries*

- and many more…

Top e-business Books

- *101 Ways to Promote Your Web Site*

- *Business-to-Business Internet Marketing*

- *Marketing on the Internet*

- and many more…

Special Offers

From IBM and other *"Exploring IBM"* team members

For more information go to *www.maxpress.com/ibmpromo1*
or e-mail us at *moreinfo@maxpress.com*

Disclaimer

The purchase of computer software or hardware is an important and costly business decision. While the author and publisher of this book have made reasonable efforts to ensure the accuracy and timeliness of the information contained herein, the author and publisher assume no liability with respect to loss or damage caused or alleged to be caused by reliance on any information contained herein and disclaim any and all warranties, expressed or implied, as to the accuracy or reliability of said information.

This book is not intended to replace the manufacturer's product documentation or personnel in determining the specifications and capabilities of the products mentioned in this book. The manufacturer's product documentation should always be consulted, as the specifications and capabilities of computer hardware and software products are subject to frequent modification. The reader is solely responsible for the choice of computer hardware and software. All configurations and applications of computer hardware and software should be reviewed with the manufacturer's representatives prior to choosing or using any computer hardware and software.

Trademarks

The words contained in this text which are believed to be trademarked, service marked, or otherwise to hold proprietary rights have been designated as such by use of initial capitalization. No attempt has been made to designate as trademarked or service marked any personal computer words or terms in which proprietary rights might exist. Inclusion, exclusion, or definition of a word or term is not intended to affect, or to express judgment upon, the validity of legal status of any proprietary right which may be claimed for a specific word or term.

Your "Members Only" Web Site

The Internet world changes every day. That's why there is a companion Web site associated with this book. On this site you will find updates to the book and other Internet marketing resources of interest. However, you have to be a member of the "3G Marketing on the Internet Insiders Club" to gain access to this site.

When you purchased this book, you automatically became a member (in fact, that's the only way to join), so you now have full privileges. To get into the "Members Only" section, go to the Maximum Press Web site located at *www.maxpress.com* and follow the links to the companion Web site for "3G Marketing on the Internet" section. When you try to enter, you will be asked for a user ID and password. Type in the following:

- For your user ID, enter: *3gmarketing*

- For your password, enter: *lucia*

You will then be granted full access to the "Members Only" area. Visit the site often and enjoy the updates and resources with our compliments—and thanks again for buying the book. We ask that you not share the user ID and password for this site with anyone else.

Table of Contents

Chapter 4:
Starting with the Foundation—Your Web Site   73

Chapter 5:
Campaign Execution   93

Chapter 6:
Web Analytics—Learn from the Past, Change the Future 139

Chapter 7:
Final Thoughts   168

1

Industry Overview—
A Look at the Internet

You're reading this book because you want to know how it can benefit your business. Perhaps you want to sell your products online, generate more leads for your sales team, provide exceptional customer service, deploy customer retention strategies, or simply generate more exposure for yourself. You may also be looking to use the Internet to provide employee training and internal communications; however, the focus of our book is on developing your business online, not employee relations, so we will stay away from this topic.

Consumers use the Internet on a regular basis and, for the most part, are quite savvy in their endeavors. Businesses are figuring out the whole Internet thing—moving away from just telling people how great they are to offering their products and services online to a welcoming marketplace. Technology continues to evolve with the explosion of the rich media consumption and wireless and mobile market growth as well as the promise of exponential growth in speed that will, in time, blow the doors off some of the barriers faced today.

The first step in your journey is to look at what's happening online today as it relates to consumers, business, and technology. The Internet has evolved into an essential place to do business, market a business, and provide customer service—and it has done so at an extremely rapid pace. In this chapter we look at:

- Consumers and the Internet

- Evolving Technology

- Business and the Internet

- Resources for Research.

Consumers and the Internet

We're a demanding bunch, aren't we? We don't care how great you are, only that we can trust you, what you can do for us, and that it can be dealt with immediately. We, as consumers, just want you to make our lives easier. We, as consumers, want to be treated like the individuals that we are.

The Internet is growing up, and so too are consumer demands. Consumers hold all the cards online as the Internet is a pull-driven medium—it is the customer who decides if he or she is going to engage you and do business with you. After all, online you're definitely not the only game in town, and customers know it.

The Internet has changed the way people behave. Look at e-mail and instant messaging—it has changed the way people communicate with each other. In the office environment, people will sooner e-mail the person sitting next to them than turn around and talk.

How Big Is the Internet Population?

The year 2005 has seen the Web grow more than any other year—even more than in the dot com boom. Supporting this, the Internet population is huge, reaching over a billion users worldwide. The following chart from content on the ClickZ site titled "Population Explosion!" (*http://www.clickz.com/stats/sectors/geographics/article.php/ 5911_151151*) provides a good look at the overall population of individual countries and the Internet user population (See Appendix A).

Your target market is out there and they're not all speaking English! There is a lot of opportunity internationally if you can effectively overcome language and cultural barriers. In fact, English-speaking Internet users represent just over 30 percent of the global Internet population. See Figure 1.1 titled "The Top Ten Languages Used on the Web" (*http://www.internetworldstats.com/stats7.htm*) for a look at leading online languages.

Globally, people use the Internet for different reasons. The research resources found later in this chapter have been included to help you drill down more to learn about your target market. In the next chapter we cover

Top Ten Languages in the Internet	Internet Users, by Language	Penetration (% Population)	World Population Estimate for Language	Language as % of Total Internet Users
English	303,132,279	27.4 %	1,107,807,851	31.7 %
Chinese	124,301,513	9.3 %	1,329,801,131	13.0 %
Japanese	78,050,000	60.9 %	128,137,485	8.1 %
Spanish	60,865,718	15.6 %	389,587,559	6.4 %
German	55,183,395	57.4 %	96,141,368	5.8 %
French	39,964,100	10.7 %	374,555,140	4.2 %
Korean	32,570,000	44.6 %	73,044,495	3.4 %
Italian	28,870,000	49.3 %	58,608,565	3.0 %
Portuguese	28,792,000	12.6 %	227,628,673	3.0 %
Dutch	14,655,328	60.5 %	24,224,721	1.6 %
TOP TEN LANGUAGES	766,384,333	20.1 %	3,809,536,987	80.0 %
Rest of the Languages	191,369,339	7.3 %	2,610,565,735	20.0 %
WORLD TOTAL	957,753,672	14.9 %	6,420,102,722	100.0 %

(*) NOTES: (1) Internet Top Ten Languages Usage Stats were updated on September 30, 2005. (2) Average Penetration is the ratio between the sum of Internet users speaking a language and the total population estimate that speaks that referred language. ©Copyright 2005, Miniwatts International, Ltd. All rights reserved.

Figure 1.1. The top ten languages used on the Web.

the importance of understanding your target market to achieve the best results online.

The Internet as a Way of Life

Here in North America, the Internet has truly become a component of daily life. According to a survey conducted by Burst Media (*http://www. burstmedia.com/*), the personal computer is quickly taking over in the home as the number one source for communications and entertainment. For many, the personal computer is the first choice for listening to music, playing games, watching movies and videos, checking out the news, and doing research. People are spending less time in front of the tube and more time on their personal computers.

You can generally group how people are using the Internet into a few broad categories:

1. To get daily information such as the news, get sports scores, and compare products. A majority of people use a search engine every day to find something of interest.

2. To perform daily communications such as e-mail and instant messaging

3. To conduct daily transactions such as their banking online and to make purchases

4. For daily entertainment such as listening to music, watching videos, and playing games.

Let's take a look at some popular online activities of Internet users in the United States according to a recent report published by the Pew Internet & American Life Project addressing the mainstreaming of online life (Figure 1.2). You can download a free copy of the full report at this URL: *http://www.pewinternet.org/PPF/r/148/report_display.asp*.

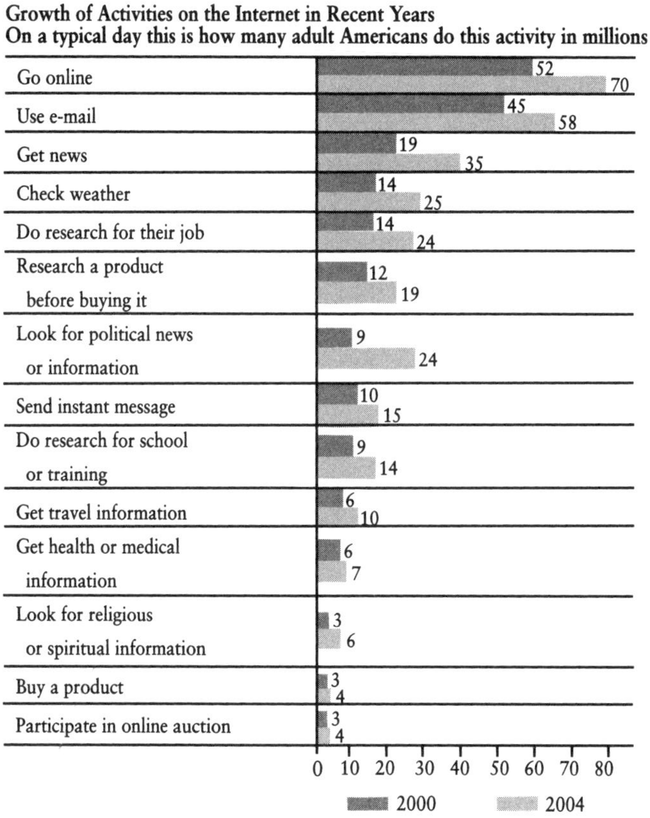

Growth of Activities on the Internet in Recent Years
On a typical day this is how many adult Americans do this activity in millions

Activity	2000	2004
Go online	52	70
Use e-mail	45	58
Get news	19	35
Check weather	14	25
Do research for their job	14	24
Research a product before buying it	12	19
Look for political news or information	9	24
Send instant message	10	15
Do research for school or training	9	14
Get travel information	6	10
Get health or medical information	6	7
Look for religious or spiritual information	3	6
Buy a product	3	4
Participate in online auction	3	4

0 10 20 30 40 50 60 70 80

■ 2000   ■ 2004

Figure 1.2. Daily activities of Internet users in the United States.

Behavior differs from gender to age to culture, and so on. Youth are more into music and games. Women more often seek health and religious information than men. Women also use the Internet to find local stores where they can purchase a product and are more likely to buy gift cards than men. There is a wealth of information out there to help you learn about your target market and who is online. Figure 1.3, from the same Pew Internet & American Life Project, outlines some of the differences in the target market of the U.S. Internet user base.

Everyone is different. Remember that. Localization and personalization in a customer-driven environment can increase the effectiveness of your online efforts because you're giving the customers what they want and you're treating them like the unique individuals they are.

The Internet is changing consumer behavior. One need look no further than the travel industry where word of mouth as the source for travel recommendations has now been replaced by the Internet as the first place people turn, in at least a dozen countries. It's not just happening in the travel industry. Across the board, people are turning to the Internet more often to conduct product research before making their next purchase. They're out there looking for the best price, comparing features, looking up reviews, researching where to buy that is closest to them, and buying online. More knowledge means more power to the consumer!

Use of the Internet for just about everything, including e-commerce, continues to grow and will continue to do so. Privacy and security continue to be the big hurdles for consumers as they relate to making purchases online. E-mail continues to be the "killer app" of the Web. A smart business stays on top of changing consumer behavior.

I Want What I Want and I Won't Have It Any Other Way

Today's Internet user is much more savvy than those of years past. People filter out unwanted material and pay attention to only what they care about. People frequently block pop-up ads, block unwanted e-mail, subscribe to niche content that just relates to their interests, and use personalization features on Web sites to weed out content that is irrelevant to them.

Today's Internet user is much more willing to vocalize his or her opinions, and we have seen the birth of the "prosumer" where people are getting involved in the customization and creation of products unique to their own needs. Again, it's all about understanding the uniqueness of individuals and giving them what they want—exactly what they want. This relates directly to Web sites that let customers personalize their experience too.

Different People Use the Internet in Different Ways

Men are more likely than women to do these activities online	Men	Women
Get news	77%	66%
Buy travel services or make reservation	60%	51%
Check sports scores and information	59%	27%
Get political news	57%	42%
Participate in online auction	28%	18%
Create content for the Internet	25%	16%
Download music files	18%	11%
Buy/sell stocks, bonds, mutual funds	16%	9%
Women are more likely than men to do these activities online	**Women**	**Men**
Get health information	85%	75%
Get spiritual and religious information	73%	56%
Use support-group Web sites	63%	46%
Online whites are more likely than minorities to do these activities	**Whites**	**Minorities**
Buy a product	63%	53%
Participate in online auction	24%	16%
African-Americans are more likely than whites to do these activities online	**Blacks**	**Whites**
Do research for school or job training	71%	58%
Look for information about a new job	61%	38%
Listen to music online	46%	30%
Download music files	25%	13%
Hispanics are more likely than non-hispanic whites to do these activities online	**Hispanics**	**Whites**
Look for new job information	61%	38%
Listen to music online	46%	30%
Young Internet users (ages 18-29) are more likely than others to do this	**Young Internet Users**	**30+**
Research for school or job training	76%	48%
Look for new job information	65%	31%
Use instant messaging	59%	33%
Listen to music online	53%	27%
Look up sports scores and information	51%	37%
Look for information about a place to live	43%	27%
Download music files	28%	11%
Share files from my computer	27%	17%
Log on using a wireless device	26%	13%
Use dating Web sites	16%	5%
Online Seniors (65+) are more likely than young Internet users to do this	**Seniors**	**18-29**
Use e-mail	96%	91%
Online middle-aged (30-64) are more likely than the young or Seniors to do this	**Middle-aged**	**Younger & Older Users**
Research a product or service	81%	71%
Look for health and medical information	70%	57%
Do work-related research	56%	38%

Figure 1.3. Different people use the Internet in different ways.

Did you know there is a community of people who have an affinity for a discontinued line of Pyrex coffee pots? You bet there is. The rapid adoption of peer-to-peer communications such as instant messaging, e-mails, and blogs has spawned all kinds of niche communities based around a shared interest.

As a business, your job to market to and communicate with your target audience has become more challenging and at the same time more exciting. Online, the customer is the one with total control. He or she knows you're not the only game in town and won't think twice about going elsewhere to get exactly what he or she wants.

Embracing Broadband

In the United States, we are approaching the 50 percent penetration mark for broadband connectivity. This means much more than high-speed Internet access; it means a much better user experience online with fewer limitations.

Broadband access is mainstream and continues to rapidly expand. According to eMarketer's "North America Broadband" report published in March 2005, it is expected that there will be approximately 70 million households with broadband Internet access in North America by 2008. Figure 1.4 shows the current status of broadband access in North America as well as predicted growth. With the expansion of high-speed Internet access comes the freedom to design more demanding and visually appealing Web sites to meet the demands of the target market. In fact, the Interactive Advertising Bureau has recently increased file size standards.

Why does the growth of broadband matter? It too is changing the behavior of Internet users from how they socialize to how they shop. A majority of purchases made online are made by broadband users. They tend to spend more time online and connect to the Internet more often than dial-up users.

Broadband Households in North America, by Country, 2004-2008 (in millions and CAGR)

	2004	2005	2006	2007	2008	CAGR
Canada	5.3	6.1	606	7.1	7.5	9.1%
U.S.	34.3	42.3	51.1	60.4	69.4	19.3%
North America	39.6	48.4	57.7	67.5	76.9	18.0%

Source: eMarketer, February 2005
062966   ©2005 eMarketer, Inc.   www.eMarketer.com

Figure 1.4. Broadband households in North America (*http://www.emarketer.com/ Report.aspx?bband_mar05*).

"Why?" you might ask. Broadband simply delivers a faster and overall more satisfying experience online.

There are predictions that within the next five years there will be over a half billion broadband users globally.

Evolving Technology

We see personal computer functionality appearing in other home appliances now. The line is blurring, and as we progress you will see more centralization as what once were several appliances will now be integrated into one. The Pioneer VSX-74TXVi Digital Surround Receiver is able to communicate with Apple's iPod, just like a personal computer would. You're also seeing home entertainment systems made available with Windows Media Center embedded. Digital cameras, MP3 players, printers, handheld devices, cellular telephones, GPS devices, digital camcorders, video game consoles, home entertainment systems, televisions, personal computers, and so on, are all becoming networkable and are sharing functionality. We see this already.

Cell phones provide a great example of converging technologies. The Nokia 9210i Communicator offers most common features of a desktop PC, including:

- Cellular mobile phone connectivity

- Desk application with background images and links

- Messaging technology SMS, fax, and e-mail

- Internet access using Web and WAP

- Address book

- Personal calendar

- Word processor, spreadsheet, presentation viewer, and file manager

- Extras such as a calculator, clock, digital camera connectivity, fax modem, music player, etc.

Needless to say, mobile devices have come a long way, and they are only expected to improve in terms of functionality and options that are available to the end user. It will be interesting to see where today's technology suppliers take us.

Interestingly enough, 2005 has also been the largest year of growth for wireless subscribers ever according to CTIA—The Wireless Association (*http://www.ctia.org/*). The following chart in Figure 1.5 published by the Computer Industry Almanac (*http://www.c-i-a.com/pr0905.htm*) shows the total global wireless subscriber population breaking through the 2 billion mark!

Get ready for wireless Web for the masses. Technology will continue to converge, blurring the lines between appliances. As technology evolves, there will be more uses for the Internet and more points of connectivity for the consumer, helping to further ingrain online life into daily routine.

As a business, the evolution of technology presents new challenges. For example, mobile devices are much smaller and people behave differently when using the Internet on them. People tend to scroll less and avoid material that has large images, which means that new content has to be tailored specifically to appeal to the mobile user.

Changing technologies will also draw new lines in the battlefield. We're seeing it as telecoms and cable providers encroach on each other's territories with Internet and communication services such as voice-over IP and broadband Internet connection services.

Top 15 Countries in Cellular Subscribers

Year-end 2005:	Cellular Subscribers (#M)	Share %
1. China	398	19.3
2. USA	202	9.9
3. Russia	115	5.6
4. Japan	95	4.6
5. Brazil	86	4.1
6. India	79	3.8
7. Germany	73	3.5
8. Italy	59	2.9
9. UK	58	2.8
10. France	47	2.3
11. Mexico	46	2.2
12. Turkey	40	1.9
13. Spain	39	1.9
14. South Korea	38	1.8
15. Indonesia	38	1.8
Top 15 Countries	1,414	68.5
Worldwide Total	2,065	100

Figure 1.5. Top 15 countries in cellular subscribers.

Business and the Internet

It's a world of opportunity out there for businesses smart enough to take advantage of it. Businesses are learning how to make money online, consumers are receptive to doing business online, and technology is making life easier as well as less expensive to accomplish what would have seemed like a dream only a couple years ago.

Businesses are using the Internet to get leads, sell their wares, provide customer service, market their business, and more. A recent study by well-known hosting company Interland (*http://www.interland.com/*) uncovered that 69 percent of small businesses defined the Internet as critical in driving business. In that same study, almost all companies said the Internet is very or somewhat important to driving business.

We are at a stage now where having an online presence is a necessity for businesses to compete today. Businesses are making money online and are not just spending it on SuperBowl ads.

Advertising Online

Online advertising works, and it is becoming big business. Searching is expected to exceed outdoor advertising in the United States within a few months, and in the United Kingdom it already has.

Much of the advertising dollars spent online seem to be on travel, health, reference, and lifestyle/news/entertainment Web sites. Advertisers are getting much smarter about their initiatives and are targeting people based on behavior to increase response rates. We said previously that not everyone is the same, and advertisers are beginning to address this.

In the United States, companies are expected to devote between 4 and 5 percent of their total advertising budget to online initiatives in the coming year, according to recent eMarketer (*http://www.emarketer.com/*) data for advertising spending (Figure 1.6). Spending on online advertising as a percentage of total advertising is growing.

Where are businesses spending their advertising dollars and what is working? The following charts (Figures 1.7 and 1.8) presented by eMarketer help shed some light on the subject. Companies are spending more money on almost all types of online advertising. E-mail marketing and search engine placement are particularly big drivers for small to medium-sized businesses.

Companies are aware of the importance of the Internet to their business, and trends indicate that they are investing more in advertising and in technology to grow online. It's all about the return on investment.

U.S. Online and Total Media Advertising Spending, 2001-2008 (in billions and online as a % of total media spending)

Year	Online	Total	Online as % of total
2001	$7.1	$231.3	3.1%
2002	$6.0	$236.9	2.5%
2003	$7.3	$245.5	3.0%
2004	$9.5	$264.2	3.6%
2005	$11.5	$278.5	4.1%
2006	$13.4	$291.0	4.6%
2007	$15.6	$302	5.2%
2008	$17.6	$307.0	5.7%

Note: eMarketer benchmarks its online ad spending projection against the Interactive Advertising Bureau (IAB)/PricewaterhouseCoopers (PWC) data, for which the last full year measured was 2003; eMarketer benchmarks its US total media ad spending projection against the Universal McCann data; for which the last full year measured was 2004
Source: eMarketer, February 2005
062766 ©2004 eMarketer, Inc.   www.eMarketer.com

Figure 1.6. Spending on online advertising.

U.S. Online Advertising Spending, by format, 2002-2008 (as a % increase/decrease vs. prior year)

	2002	2003	2004	2005	2006	2007	2008
Display Ads	-30.2%	-13.5%	15.2%	14.5%	6.5%	20.1%	9.1%
Sponsorship	-42.2%	-33.5%	17.7%	14.3%	16.5%	16.4%	12.8%
Paid Search	210.5%	174.3%	51.3%	22.5%	17.9%	17.8%	12.8%
Classified	-19.4%	37.0%	30.7%	24.6%	16.5%	13.1%	9.5%
Rich Media*	69.9%	93.5%	38.9%	35.3%	28.8%	27.5%	22.6%
Interstitials*	12.3%	-39.5%	-	-	-	-	-
E-mail	22.9%	-9.3%	-12.8%	21.1%	16.5%	-12.7%	12.8%
Slotting Fees	-13.1%	-54.7%	8.9%	-3.2%	16.5%	-41.8%	12.8%
Referrals	-57.9%	20.9%	161.5%	21.1%	16.5%	16.4%	12.8%
Total	**-15.8%**	**20.9%**	**30.7%**	**21.1%**	**16.5%**	**16.4%**	**12.8%**

*Note: eMarketer benchmarks its U.S. online ad spending projections against the Interactive Advertising Bureau (IAB)/PricewaterhouseCoopers (PWC) data, for which the last full year measured was 2003; *as of 2004, the Rich Media category includes interstitials*
Source: eMarketer, February 2005
062887 ©2004 eMarketer, Inc.   www.eMarketer.com

Figure 1.7. Advertising spending by format.

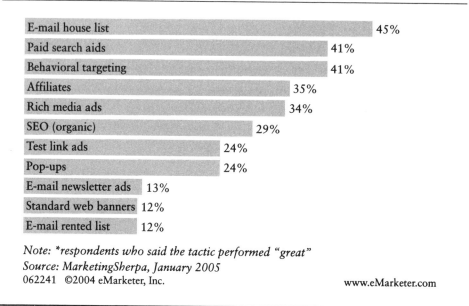

Top Performing Online Advertising Tactics*, according to AD: TECH Attendees, December 2004 (as a % of respondents)

E-mail house list	45%
Paid search aids	41%
Behavioral targeting	41%
Affiliates	35%
Rich media ads	34%
SEO (organic)	29%
Test link ads	24%
Pop-ups	24%
E-mail newsletter ads	13%
Standard web banners	12%
E-mail rented list	12%

Note: *respondents who said the tactic performed "great"
Source: MarketingSherpa, January 2005
062241   ©2004 eMarketer, Inc.   www.eMarketer.com

Figure 1.8.   Advertising tactics that work well.

Resources for Research

New statistics and information are being released all the time that are useful to the company doing business online. By the time this book goes to print, some of the statistics will be dated. It is up to you to keep yourself in the know. Here are a few of our favorite resources—some free, some not.

These sites are great for keeping up to date with the latest trends, and most have newsletters so the information can be delivered directly to your inbox.

eMarketer (*http://www.emarketer.com*)—Many of the tables and statistics you see in this book come from eMarketer. They are a great resource for e-business statistics, demographics, Internet usage, and research. They have a free newsletter you can subscribe to and offer paid services in the form of online database subscriptions and market research reports.

ClickZ Stats (*http://www.clickz.com/stats*)—ClickZ represents a huge collection of online statistics and research from many sources and on many categories including:

- Advertising/marketing

- B2B

- Broadband

- Demographics

- Education

- E-mail/spam

- Entertainment

- Finance

- Geographics

- Government/politics

- Hardware

- Healthcare

- Professional

- Retailing

- Search tools

- Security issues

- Small/medium enterprises

- Software/IT

- Traffic patterns

- Travel

- Wireless.

You can subscribe to ClickZ to receive regular updates by e-mail.

MarketingVOX (*http:// www.marketingvox.com*)—Another awesome publication is MarketingVOX. If you're responsible in some fashion for online marketing in your organization, you should subscribe now to their newsletter or RSS feed for online marketing and e-marketing news.

W3Schools Browser Statistics (*http://www.w3schools.com/browsers/browsers_stats.asp*)—A free resource from W3Schools Browser Statistics, outlines popular browsers, operating systems, color depth, and screen resolutions of Internet users.

The Pew Internet & American Life Project *(http:// www.pewinternet.org)*—Research that delves into how the Internet impacts life and society can be found at The Pew Internet & American Life Project. Reports are released regularly, and you can subscribe to be notified by e-mail of when they are available.

This is just a small sampling of sites you can use for market research. Not everyone can spend thousands of dollars on a single study, so we appreciate anything we can get for free!

Industry analysts often offer some insight for free if you know where to look for it. Here are some of the big industry analysts. Check out their sites when doing your research. Jupiter Research, for example, offers free Webinars on their Web site as well as blogs from their analysts.

- Jupiter Research, *http://www.jupiterresearch.com*

- Gartner, *http://www.gartner.com*

- Forrester Research, *http://www.forrester.com*

- ComScore MediaMetrix, *http://www.comscore.com*

- Nielsen/NetRatings, *http://www.netratings.com*

- Vividence, *http://www.vividence.com*.

Closing Comments

It's a 3G world and times are changing. Consumer expectations are through the roof and you must deliver. Web sites have rapidly gone from brochureware to essential customer touch points.

Figure 1.9. Audi's Web site in 1996.

For example, in the car industry the Internet has become a huge factor for potential buyers. People are turning to the Internet to do in-depth vehicle research before ever stepping foot in a dealer; when they come, they're coming with a lot more ammo.

Look at Audi's Web site from nearly a decade ago in the following figure (Figure 1.9). Not much to it at all because a decade ago it was not considered a pivotal factor for doing business.

Look at Audi's Web site today in Figure 1.10. Audi recognizes that consumers are doing extensive research online. In fact, according to a new study by J.D. Power and Associates (*http://www.jdpower.com*), almost 70 percent of new-car buyers use the Internet during the vehicle buying process. Audi has country-specific Web sites; potential customers can build their own vehicle online, evaluate financing options, shop the online store for clothes and car accessories, make contact with a sales representative in the local area, and of course view very detailed, interactive specifications on each vehicle that includes movies that walk the potential customer through different aspects of a vehicle. It's all about the customer experience, and Audi knows what it takes to get people into the dealerships.

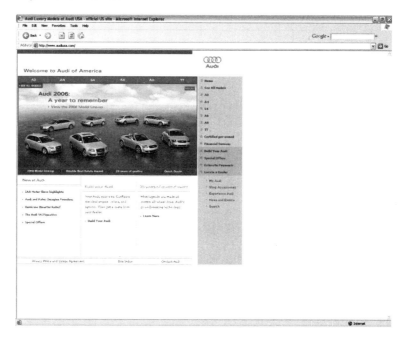

Figure 1.10.   Audi's Web site going into 2006.

While we will not see a revolution in the heart of the Internet, we will continue to see rapid evolution that will open the door to new opportunities. Some businesses choose to fight change, but successful businesses are the ones that embrace change and are proactive in keeping pace with changing consumer demands. The Internet will continue to grow; it will become faster, it will become cheaper, and it will become smarter.

As a business going into a 3G environment, you need to be prepared to keep on top of ever-changing consumer demands, and you must take online marketing and using your Web site as a point of business seriously to succeed. In the coming sections of this book, we help lay out your plan to achieve success online. Good luck!

The Internet is not going away any time soon; it's going to evolve and become more ingrained in all our lives.

2

Understanding Your Environment

One of the biggest oversights that businesses make when developing their online marketing strategy is that they do not think five steps ahead. Many businesses continuously rush into the implementation process of their online marketing and Web site strategy with no clear plan, documented objectives, or measurement guidelines in place so that they are often left scratching their heads at the end of the day saying, "Why did we do that?" That's a great question! Why did you implement an email marketing campaign? Why do you participate in PPC campaigns? Why do you continuously update your Web site? You do this because you understand your business, your objectives, and what you want the Web to do for you. You've thought things through; you have targets and a means to measure your performance.

In this section of *3G Marketing on the Internet,* we cover the following topics:

- Long term planning and your Web site strategy

- Understanding your objectives

- Identifying your target market

- Understanding the user

- What exactly are you promoting?

- Extending the reach of your brand online

- Consistently positioning your offerings

- Staying on top of the competition

- Being aware of the macro and micro environmental landscape

- Determining your budget.

Long Term Planning and Your Web Site Strategy

A well-planned Internet marketing strategy distinguishes those businesses that are committed to the long-term potential of the medium from those who are simply marketing online because the market says they should. Typically, the latter can easily be detected. I am sure you've stumbled across a Web site that is nothing more than an electronic brochure—a site that does not communicate the promise of the brand to the target market or a site that is stamped "Last Updated . . ." only to display a date one or two years prior to your visit (or more.) These are examples of businesses that have yet to fully embrace the potential of the Internet and how it can not only grow their business, but also reach more users in a more cost-effective manner.

Planning plays a critical role in the success of your Internet marketing strategy with regard to your Web site itself, the online communication channels that you choose, and how you actually execute each campaign you launch to your target market. Those businesses that are capitalizing on the mainstream use of the Internet are those that plan their Internet strategies well in advance. For example, research reveals that the average online marketer that is using targeted PPC campaigns or organic optimization as a means of driving traffic to their Web site are dedicating on average 36 percent of their total online advertising budget to the medium. That represents 15 percent of their total online/offline advertising budget. Does this seem like a surprise? It shouldn't. It's not unrealistic for search engine exposure to be able to represent 60 to 80 percent of a Web site's total traffic.

A common question that arises is, "How do you plan your Internet strategy in a world where technology is changing constantly?" This is a somewhat valid question. Yes, technology changes, but this does not affect only your Internet strategy; it affects every facet of your business. The best way to answer the question is with the following question: "How do you plan to grow your business?" If you don't have an answer to this question, you have

Figure 2.1. The "foundation" of your online marketing strategy.

a bigger issue and probably should be reading a book on developing a business strategy. More importantly, if the Internet (or related technologies) is not a part of how you plan to grow your business, you should definitely keep reading this book.

So how do you typically plan to manage the growth of your business? For starters, you forecast to the best of your ability where your business will be six months, one year, two years from now, and so on, and you develop a strategy to facilitate this growth both from a sales and a delivery point of view. How does this relate to the Internet? Well, your Web site and Internet strategy should be flexible enough to grow with your business without having to start from scratch every time your business reaches a new milestone.

Figure 2.1 illustrates what we refer to as "the foundation" for all Web site activities. If you don't take the foundation into account, then the structure of your entire online marketing strategy will fall to pieces. The key components of your foundation include:

- Understanding your primary online marketing objectives

- Identifying your primary and secondary target market segments

- Having a clear understanding of what you're promoting on your site.

Understanding Your Objectives

Understanding what you are trying to achieve online plays a critical role in the planning process for your Web site and your overall online marketing strategy. It seems like a simple concept, doesn't it? I mean, why would you build a Web site if you didn't understand what you want it to do? Well, the problem is that even in this day and age, many businesses are developing their online presence simply because it's just one of those things that businesses need to do. These businesses build Web sites that are online brochures for their business with little or no thought about their customers or what they want their site to achieve.

Any online marketing activities, whether it is the development of your Web site or planning sessions for an online campaign, should begin by documenting the specific primary objectives for the activity. Typically it boils down to one primary objective that is common across any business—revenue generation. But what does this really mean? Do you have to sell products online to generate revenue for your business, or can you simply use the site to qualify sales leads for your internal sales department? Overall there are many different online marketing objectives for a company Web site or a specific campaign. People tend to label their objectives simply as "revenue generation" as opposed to breaking down the objective into more specific terms. Below is a list of common online marketing objectives:

- Generate increased brand awareness

- Generate and qualify leads for the internal sales department

- Increase revenue as a result of online sales

- Provide increased customer service by providing the Web user with more self-service tools and information

- Increase customer retention

- Decrease internal costs by streamlining the share of information online.

To illustrate the importance of defining precise online objectives, consider the following. Throughout the years many businesses have made Web site traffic their primary objective and have invested heavily into various means of getting traffic to their Web sites. These businesses followed the philosophy that traffic would result in increased sales. Well, how can you judge the success of your online activities if your whole campaign is based on a vague objective? Simply generating traffic is not tied to a financial objective of any sort, so how can one judge the success of the campaign with such a loose goal in mind? Instead, stating an objective like "achieving a cost per customer acquisition of $15 as a result of a targeted PPC advertising campaign" helps a business to put a targeted, measurable objective on a particular activity.

Without defining precise objectives for your online activities, it is nearly impossible to gauge success of any sort. Using the example above, you could drive waves of traffic to your Web site, but what if the medium you selected wasn't right for your business and the traffic you received was not a targeted visitor at all? You received lots of traffic, yes, but you also wasted time and money and had a poor ROI as a result. This often forces businesses to make subjective decisions about the success of the campaign or the effectiveness of the medium in general, but the truth of the matter is that it's not fair to state whether something is a failure or success unless you can really prove it. By defining objectives that are measurable, businesses can determine if a campaign works or doesn't work. If it works, you can continue to implement such campaigns, and if it doesn't work, you can tweak your approach and test it again. The key lesson here is to make all of your objectives measurable.

Identifying Your Target Market

As important as it is for you to understand what you are trying to accomplish online, it is equally important to thoroughly understand with whom you are trying to communicate. Who is your target market online? The typical response is "our customers." Even in today's connected business environment, people don't step back to think about the different segments of your target market who could visit your Web site. Of course you're trying to communicate with your customers—that's a given.

Like most businesses, you probably have different segments of your customer base. It can be as simple as segmenting existing customers from prospective customers. Once you bring a prospective customer to your Web site, you have to ensure that everything is in line from a branding perspective, that the content on your site speaks to the needs of this customer group, and that you can easily walk them through the buying process—whether it be to buy online or to complete a task of some sort to display their interest in your product or service (e.g., download a white paper on your product).

At the same time, your Web site needs to speak to your existing client base. This can include self-service tools and other customer service–oriented Web site components, special offers that are applicable only to clients, and other Web site elements that will keep your brand and your offerings in front of your existing clients. As the old saying goes, it's much easier to keep an existing client than it is to get a new one! It's a competitive world out there, and the Internet is one of the most cost-effective ways to communicate with your clients, so make sure you keep this in mind when developing both your Web site and your different online campaigns.

In addition to your current and prospective clients, you also need to step back and think of the big picture. Anyone can visit your site to learn about your organization, so it's important to think about all of the different market segments that you could touch with your Web site; this extends beyond your customers. For example, if one of your online marketing objectives is to generate increased awareness for your organization, the brand, and your product/ service offerings, then the inclusion of a robust media center or press room should be included on the Web site. The content found within this section of your Web site should be framed toward the unique interest of the press and should make it easy for the press to prepare a story on your organization.

Understanding the User

Understanding your target market also affects "how" you target your customers. It's one thing to know whom you are targeting, but if you get them to the front door and they are unable to open the door to see what's inside, what is the point? For example, according to the Pew Internet & American Life Project, 22 percent of American citizens 65 years of age and older use the Internet—a 47 percent increase between 2000 and 2004. This is a significant increase and will only continue to grow as more and more seniors embrace the Internet.

Now if you have a business that is targeting customers who fall into this category, you need to make sure that all of your customer touch points appeal to this market segment. This could be as simple as using appropriate font sizes on advertisements that you place on the Internet so that users with poor eyesight can easily read your offer and visit your site, but this is just the beginning. Once the user gets to your site, you have to make sure that everything on the site is accommodating, as many seniors will encounter different usability issues due to disabilities or sheer lack of knowledge of how the Internet works. Below is a quick list of design elements that research has proven create a more favorable experience for this market segment:

- The use of larger font sizes and the ability to scale the font size larger by simply clicking a button (see Figure 2.2)

- Increased use of image-based links that provide the user with a larger clickable area

Figure 2.2. Dell enables users to increase font size by selecting the "Large Text" option, which is present on every page of the Web site.

- Clear calls to action that explain why a user should click on a particular button and what is going to happen when he or she does (e.g., Click here to download your free e-book)

- Easy-to-use navigation systems that provide the user with clearly labeled navigation options in an open list structure as opposed to drop-down menus, hidden layers of navigation, and excessive cross-linking

- Eliminating the need for any type of horizontal scrolling in smaller pop-up windows that contain important information and open new windows to be large enough to minimize vertical scrolling—something that proves particularly difficult when using larger font sizes.

The intention of this example is not to teach you how to market to seniors, or to any particular market segment for that matter. Complete books have been written on that subject matter. The intention of the example is to illustrate how it is important to understand how your target market thinks and what will encourage users to interact with your business online. As you can see, marketing to seniors can require a significant amount of hand holding and customization that other segments of your customer base may not require. This leads many businesses to develop and market separate mini-sites that are designed to tailor to the unique needs of this market segment, while they have another site that is marketed to the younger, more Internet savvy segment of their customer base.

Understanding not only whom you are targeting but how they work is critical to online success. Internet users are picky, and they have a lot of options available to them online, so it's important that you give them what they want. If you do, you will ensure that they remember the experience that they have had with your business, which will result in repeat business and more exposure for your business as a whole.

What Exactly Are You Promoting?

It sounds like a silly concept, doesn't it? I mean, it's your business, so you know your own products or services inside out, right? It's amazing how many businesses get caught up in the design process of their Internet presence and lose sight of what it is that they are actually promoting online. Quite often, businesses get so involved in wondering how their Web site looks that they actually forget about what it is they are promoting, whom they are targeting, and why they are even promoting it online in the first place. Can you see how the key components of the foundation work together?

So, what are you promoting? Is it simply your products/services? Yes, this is what you want your customers to purchase, but selling to someone online is a lot different from selling to someone face to face. There are so many factors that play an influential role in encouraging an online user to take the next step and engage your business and its offerings. Each of these factors typically tie into your most fundamental (and often overlooked) online objectives.

To illustrate, let's assume that you are promoting Product X, which is a highly specialized piece of equipment with a hefty price tag. You are not the only competitor in the market that offers Product X, but your version of the product is slightly different from the rest. So why should someone buy your product? This is where you have to wrap your head around what you are promoting, while differentiating it from the other options that users have within the marketplace.

Well, how do you do this? You have to tell the user a story of why your product is superior. Is there a specific process that your company follows when developing Product X? Do the materials of your product make it superior? Yes, these are all great points to make, but to truly sell your story you need to explain what is in it for the user. If users are looking to buy your product, they have a pain that they are looking for you to relieve (not in the literal sense). Tell them why they should buy your product. Don't just say, "Here it is, buy it!" Through telling the right story, you can accomplish a number of high-level online objectives outside of simply generating revenue as a result of product sales, which include:

- Properly positioning your products/services in the marketplace

- Increased brand awareness for your business

- Extending the promise of your brand and your story beyond the Web. (This will be covered in the next section of this chapter.)

At this point, the extent to which "the foundation" of your online strategy plays should be clear. Without setting measurable objectives, there is really no point in engaging in any online marketing activities. You can drive an endless amount of traffic to your Web site, but if the traffic isn't targeted and you don't tell the right story to your different target market segments, then the likelihood that you will convert a prospect to a buyer decreases significantly. And how do you properly tell the story of your product or service? You have to understand it inside and out, in relation to your competition, and capitalize on any unique attributes of what you're offering that will distinguish you from your competition.

Throughout the rest of this book, all techniques, processes, and strategies relate back to this foundation. As simple as this may seem, these three components drive your entire online marketing strategy, including your Web site, Internet marketing campaigns, and benchmarks for measurement. When one item is overlooked or misinterpreted by a business, this oversight will be reflected in the results once your strategy is executed.

Extending the Reach of Your Brand Online

The Internet provides businesses with a dynamite opportunity to extend their reach to new users and prospective clients, all in a cost-effective environment. With approximately 137.54 million Internet users in the United States alone, the Internet enables businesses to reach more people more frequently, which results in greater brand awareness among your target audience for those businesses that carefully plan and implement their online marketing strategy.

The challenge that businesses face is actually connecting with their target market. Throughout the years, an endless amount of inquiries have filtered into our consulting business with the infamous tale of high traffic and no conversion. Many businesses think that each and every online communication channel that is available is appropriate for their business; thus, they believe that they need to cover all avenues in order to succeed online. Is this the case? Not at all. In fact, later in this book we are going to cover how you can select appropriate communication channels for your business.

The point is that the Internet provides businesses with a tremendous opportunity to reach new clients at a fraction of the cost of traditional offline marketing campaigns. Through taking the appropriate steps to orient yourself with your current environment while crafting a strategy to reach your target market through electronic media, you will reach your market, and once you get them to your Web site the first time, you have to keep bringing them back. Nobody wants a one-hit client—you want a greater share of wallet from each of your customers; therefore, it is important to implement the appropriate tools and techniques to ensure that once you get a customer, you continue to retain him or her.

Consistently Positioning Your Offerings

Businesses spend a significant amount of time and resources developing their offline marketing plan, messaging, and tonality of every marketing piece that is made available to the public. What's amusing is that many businesses don't devote the same amount of effort into the messaging of their online marketing collateral. It's crucial that your customers are presented with a consistent message and style across all customer touch points. To be most effective, your company's Web site, online advertising creative, and messaging used in your copy should be consistent with your overall marketing plan. This goes for everything from the creative that is executed on your site, wording in your online ads, the copy used on your site, to messaging used on targeted landing pages. By aligning your online and offline marketing efforts, you will better achieve your overall business objectives.

Having stated the above, it's important to remember that you shouldn't simply reuse copy that is used in your offline collateral online. Remember, you're driving your customers to the Web site for a reason, whether that is to enter a contest, purchase a product, or simply download a white paper. Web copy is not the same as copy used in a corporate brochure. (More on writing for the Web will be covered later in this book.) The point is that if you direct users to your Web site from a business card, television commercial, or billboard, they perceive a value for visiting your site. They don't want to visit the site to simply see the same thing. Yes, the style and tonality of the messaging should be consistent, but don't say the same thing twice. You've got them to your front door; it's time to close the deal.

Learn From Your Customers

The easiest way to learn how to make your products or services more appealing to your target market is to learn from those who have already been exposed to your offerings. In the offline world, this would result in numerous time-intensive focus groups, annoying customer surveys, and open-ended interviews. Although these techniques are a great way to study your customer base, they also are time-intensive, are costly, and often end up inconveniencing your customers. In today's "wired world" you not only can reach more customers in a cost-effective manner, but you can also enable users to provide their feedback at their convenience without the pressure of answering questions in high-pressure environments such as a one-on-one interview.

How can feedback from your clients help you with planning your strategy? Well, it's just as important to know why users purchase your products or services as it is to know how to get them to your offerings. For example, let's take Amos Pewter (*www.amospewter.com*), one of the leading retailers of hand crafted pewter products and collectibles. Amos Pewter sells pewter products of various design themes, purposes, and prices. Typically businesses will just build their e-commerce Web site, place their products on the site under logical navigation categories, and launch their Web site hoping that their customers will find the products they want in their storefront and will make an online purchase.

Is this the best way to present products online? It is true that you can take this approach; in fact, many businesses have profited from this approach. However, by truly understanding your customers, you can optimize their online shopping experience by providing users with multiple ways to find their desired products on your Web site. How do you do this? By studying your customers' typical buying patterns. Users may purchase products for a number of different reasons or may seek out product information by a number of different means, so it's important for you to understand those reasons while planning your marketing strategy.

For example, Amos Pewter presents their products to their customers under logical categories; however, their sales reports indicated that sales spike during a given holiday, thus it made sense to also include a "reasons to buy" or "gift-giving occasions" section on the site, as it speaks to the needs of your customers (see Figure 2.3). Providing users with multiple

Figure 2.3.   Amos Pewter (*www.amospewter.com*) spends a significant amount of time learning from its customers and presenting its online shopping experience based on its customers' shopping habits.

ways to access your products based on their purchase behavior will result in increased sales for your business. This theory can be applied to all businesses; thus, it is critical that a behavioral analysis of some sort take place prior to planning your strategy.

Staying on Top of the Competition

Staying on top of what your competition is doing in the industry is vital to the success of your business. The moment you stop monitoring what your competition is doing is the moment your business risks falling behind in the industry. The same theory applies to your Web site and online marketing strategy. In order to stay ahead on the Web, you should review competing sites to see what they are doing. What type of content are they providing? What techniques are they using to communicate with their (and your) target audience? How are they organizing content? What type of repeat-traffic-generating elements are they using? Are they offering any unique services via their Web site that are giving them a competitive edge? If you don't plan your online strategy without taking the competition into consideration, you are headed down the wrong path before you even get started. Having said that, you should constantly monitor your competitive landscape to ensure that you stay ahead of the competitive curve.

Being Aware of the Macro and Micro Environmental Landscape

When planning your business strategy, you always have to analyze your macroenvironment and microenvironment; this goes without saying. So why should it be any different when planning your online marketing strategy? Your online marketing strategy is only an extension of your business's overall marketing plan, and thus it should be developed in conjunction with the rest of your marketing plans for the business.

We've already touched on a few key issues that should be considered that relate to this topic: competition, customers, and the aging population as ex-

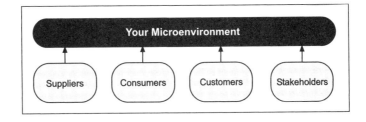

Figure 2.4. A basic overview of your microenvironment.

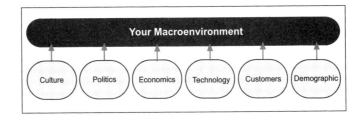

Figure 2.5. A basic overview of your macroenvironment.

amples. Without regurgitating something that has been written over and over again in almost every marketing book that is available, Figures 2.4 and 2.5 provide an overview of key factors to review in both your macroenvironment and microenvironment while formulating your online marketing strategy. Remember, it's important to take a holistic look at your business to understand not only your foundation, but how each and every component of your business affects your online presence.

For example, a common issue that many businesses have encountered that falls inside their microenvironment is dealing with suppliers—namely, shipping agents. When you're promoting your products online through an e-commerce storefront for the whole world to see, you are extending well beyond marketing within the regions that, for example, you covered with a traditional offline catalog. Well, now that your products can reach new geographic areas, how do you plan to fulfill orders that are generated in these areas? Do your current shipping agents reach these markets, and if they do, can they deliver products as efficiently as your current customers have grown to expect from your organization? This is a very simplistic example, yet it's something that businesses encounter all the time. If you're opening your doors to a larger audience, you'd better make sure you can support the influx in business.

Determining Your Budget

So now it's time to bring up everyone's favorite subject—the "b" word. Of course, everything you do online relates back to what you can afford to do. With that being said, the truth of the matter is that everyone cannot afford to do everything—at least, not all at once. The other reality is, like with anything, you get what you pay for. Over the years I am sure you've heard business associates boasting about how they paid close to nothing for their Web presence. We've seen so many of those Web sites over the years, too. Typically we view them with the accompanying phone call from a "soon to be" client complaining about their Web site and how it is not generating any results. We all know why they are not seeing results.

It is not our intention to dictate what your online marketing budget should be. The point is that it is critical for you to fully understand your entire environment prior to investing anything in your Web site and online marketing strategy. Once you understand where you need to be to effectively communicate with your clients, you can then prioritize these items and allocate your budget accordingly. Quite often the implementation of your full strategy has to be completed in phases that are dictated by the budget. This is fine because a phased strategy is in place to roll out the sequential phases when the budget is available. The key is that you have a "strategy" and a vision for where your business is headed online—not an ad hoc way of marketing your business online, which will result in less-than-stellar results.

There are numerous other factors that one should take into consideration when determining their online marketing budget. Consider the following points:

- *Environment:* How active is your industry in the online marketplace? For example, the travel industry is heavily involved in online advertising; thus, ad rates are likely to be higher and the overall competitive nature of the medium will increase advertising costs. If this is the case, it's critical that you research the available options to ensure that you can maximize your overall advertising budget for your clients.

- *Competition:* Staying competitive means that you have to compete aggressively with your competition. If you're in an industry where all of your key competitors are utilizing various channels and are gaining market share, you may have to have a similar online advertising budget or more just to defend your territory.

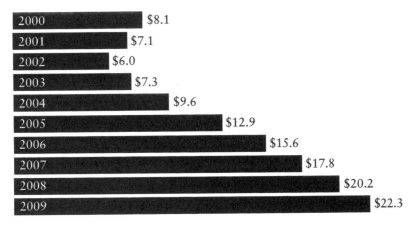

Note: eMarketer benchmarks its U.S. online ad spending projections against the Interactive Advertising Bureau (IAB) – PricewaterhouseCoopers (PWC) data, for which the last full year measured was 2004
Source: eMarketer, May 2005
064498   ©2005 eMarketer, Inc.   www.eMarketer.com

Figure 2.6.   eMarketer illustrates the consistent increase in online advertising spending.

- *Target Market:* How active is your target market? How often does your target market utilize the Internet to research products, etc.? This may seem like common sense, but if your target audience researches products more online than offline, wouldn't it make sense to scale back on your offline budgets and allocate more to online marketing?

In 2005, online ad spending in the United States alone will have surpassed $12.9 billion according to reports from eMarketer (see Figure 2.6). By 2009, companies will spend nearly $10 billion more on online advertising, reaching $22.3 billion. These statistics will continue to grow as time goes on—a sure sign that more and more businesses are turning to the Web to grow their business and to capitalize on the influx of people who are rushing to the Internet to conduct research and shop for products online.

In order to succeed online, you need to embrace the medium. Don't think of the Internet as simply an expense. Your online presence is an investment in the future of your business; thus, it shouldn't be neglected. Are there cost-effective ways to market online? Sure, but the process you follow to develop your strategy should be the same regardless. Understand your environment, your customers, and where you want the Internet to take you. Without doing so, you're two steps behind before you even get started.

3

Internet Marketing Techniques

We have made great strides in Internet marketing techniques over the last decade. The first-generation techniques were very limited. Many online marketers thought banner advertising was the way to go—and the only way to go. Back in the "olden days," banner advertising worked as a means to generate Web site traffic. A few online marketers were using Usenet Newsgroups to develop a reputation for themselves and to generate traffic for their Web sites. Very little was known about search engine ranking criteria, but then again, there was very little to know. Some of the search engines operated on a last-in first-out (LIFO) basis, meaning that as long as you re-submitted regularly, your site would stay at the top of the Search results.

The second-generation Internet marketing techniques were, and still are, varied and focused. After Web sites had been around for a few years and the novelty of just having a site wore off, the owners of the sites wanted to see results or a return on their investment. People realized that there was a Formula for e-Business Success (shameless self-promotion for another of my books). The Formula for e-Business Success is basically:

The right e-Business model

+

The right Web site

+

The right Web site traffic (and lots of it)

=

e-Business Success

In the second generation, people realized that it wasn't just any traffic that they wanted, but targeted traffic. There were many effective ways to generate targeted traffic (more shameless self-promotion for my *101 Ways to Promote Your Web Site* book). Many of these techniques are still very effective today—things like public mail list marketing, direct mail list marketing, use of signature files, newsgroup marketing, meta-index marketing, marketing through awards, media relations, e-zine marketing, Web ring marketing, and others. We won't cover these Internet marketing techniques in this book as they have been covered in-depth in *101 Ways to Promote Your Web Site,* and we want to focus our attention in this book on the third generation of Internet marketing. In this chapter, we cover:

- Search engine—organic optimization

- The importance of your link strategy

- Internet advertising—rich media

- Internet advertising—search engine

- Internet advertising—contextual advertising

- Internet advertising—behavioral advertising

- Affiliate marketing

- RSS

- Blogging

- Podcasting/videocasting

- Mobile marketing

- Viral marketing

- Autoresponder marketing

- Permission-based e-mail marketing

- VOIP.

Search Engine—Organic Optimization

Back in the "olden days," placing nice and high in the search results was not a big issue. There were few sites. In 1992 there were fewer than 20,000 domains, and the search engines had relatively primitive ranking algorithms or formulas. Many of the search engines worked on a LIFO principle, so to stay on top you re-submitted every couple of weeks. There were software tools that did the submissions and re-submissions for you that weren't rejected by the search engines.

When Google appeared in 1998, it changed the search world. People found that Google was providing much better results than the other search engines, and it quickly became the favorite of most of the online world. The reason for the better results in large part was due to the link popularity element in its algorithm. Google's premise was that if a lot of sites are providing a link to a particular site, it must be a good site; no one provides a link to a mediocre site.

The second generation brought more sophisticated algorithms and formulas. Internet marketers learned as much as they could about these algorithms and optimized pages of their Web sites accordingly. Of course, the search engines weren't releasing too much information on their formulas because that was their "Colonel Sanders recipe." If they provide their formula details to you they also provide it to their competitors.

Methodologies for optimizing your site for the search engines started to appear, and these are still relevant today. Our methodology for optimization is provided step-by-step in great detail in *101 Ways to Promote Your Web Site,* and you will find details in the Resources section of *http://www.susansweeney.com* as well as in Susan's newsletter archives on her site. In a nutshell, the methodology includes:

1. Determine the search engines you want to focus on. These usually will be the most heavily used search engines.

2. Learn as much as you can about their algorithms or formulas for ranking sites.

3. Determine the keywords and keyword phrases you want to focus on with the search engines. You will need to do a fair bit of research in this area to finalize your selection. Tools like WordTracker provide great intelligence.

4. Allocate different keywords and keyword phrases to different pages of your Web site based on the content.

5. Populate the respective pages of the site with the assigned keywords/ keyword phrases appropriately. The keywords/keyword phrases need to be included in:

   a. The domain name or file extension for that page of the site. For example, for a page that was being optimized for the term "web development," you would use *http://www.verbinteractive.com/ webdevelopment.html*

   b. The page title

   c. The text of the page. At the time of publication of this book, the keyword phrase would be included at the very beginning, the middle, and the end of the page. It would be repeated about five times and would have a keyword density of no less than 3 percent and no higher than 12 percent.

   d. In the alt tags

   e. In the headers

   f. In the keyword meta-tags

   g. In the description meta-tags

   h. Comments tag.

Online marketers were also aware of the offsite ranking criteria that were included in the formulas and, wherever possible, developed strategies to score high there as well. These elements included things like:

1. Link popularity

2. Link relevancy

3. Keyword being searched on in the text around the link

4. Click-throughs from search results and length of stay

5. Site traffic

6. Length of domain registration

7. Frequency of updates

8. Google page rank.

So here we are in the early stages of the third generation where many of the elements of generation 1 and generation 2 are still valid but they are just a part of the equation. These evolving formulas are difficult to keep current in a printed book, so I'll refer you back to the resources and newsletter archive on *http://www.susansweeney.com*. The formulas are continually being enhanced and different weighting is given to different elements in the algorithm.

The third generation search engines' algorithms continue to enhance the results provided whenever a search is performed. In the future, quite likely the results will be different for different people doing a search of the same keyword or keyword phrase. The formula will likely take into consideration things like:

- User preferences

- User past selections. If in the past you have done a number of searches for "windows" because you were doing a home renovation project and always selected the sites that related to house windows rather than the Microsoft Windows–referenced sites, the search engine would learn from your past selections and provide results related to house windows.

- Your geographic location

- Your demographic and psychographic history

- The time of the day the search was performed.

The search engines will build a profile on each user based on sites visited, sites clicked through from search results, how long he or she stayed on those sites, etc., to be able to provide the best results for you.

The search engines will also continue to weed out inappropriate sites from their databases. They are already doing a decent job on this, eliminating sites that are trying to manipulate the search results by using doorway or gateway pages, duplicate sites, link farms, multiple links with exactly the same text around the link, and other manipulative techniques.

In this third generation we certainly have seen a search explosion—we can now search for videos, images, and maps as well as search locally. Each of these can require its own strategy for organic search engine optimization.

For example, with videos, important keywords in the video filename as well as in all the appropriate places on the page that the video file is found are important for ranking consideration.

We discuss search engine advertising, sponsored listings, and programs in the Internet Advertising sections of this chapter.

The Importance of Your Link Strategy

The first generation of Internet marketing saw Web site owners work on getting linked from other sites because they saw the benefit of the traffic from those sites. Their link strategies primarily related to finding sites that related to different products or services but had the same target market as theirs and requesting a link from the site's owner. Usually reciprocal links were negotiated, placement was negotiated, and graphics and text for the links were traded.

The second generation saw link strategies get a little more sophisticated, certainly as link popularity and link relevancy became significantly prominent elements in the search engines' ranking criteria. Organizations took a very strategic approach to getting linked from as many sites as possible to improve their link popularity scores. They implemented very thorough, organized, and detailed link strategies. Two popular strategies that have been suggested in most of my books that still work well today are:

Strategy 1

1. Gather an extensive list of sites that sell to your target market along with their Web addresses.

2. Choose a link popularity tool that will give you a detailed list of all the sites that are linking to a specific Web site. There are many free tools like this on the Web; just Google "free link popularity tool" or use Google itself.

3. Enter the first Web address from Step 1 in the link popularity tool to find the sites linking to it.

4. Copy (highlight the results and press CTRL-C) and paste (CTRL-V) the results into Word, Excel, or another file you will access later.

5. Enter the next Web address from Step 1 to find the sites linking to it.

6. Copy and paste the results into the same file that you began in Step 4.

7. Repeat Steps 5 and 6 until you have found all the sites linking to your competition. When it is complete, you have your Potential Link Sites list.

8. Now develop a link request letter and keep it open on your desktop so that you can copy and paste it into an e-mail when you find a site that you'd like to have a link from.

9. Next, visit each of the potential link sites to determine whether the site is appropriate for you to be linked from. If the site is appropriate, then send your link request. If the site is not appropriate for whatever reason, delete it from your list.

10. Follow through and follow up. Follow through and provide an appropriate link to those who have agreed to a reciprocal link. Follow up to make sure that they have provided the link to your site as promised, that the link works, and that it is pointing to the correct page on your site.

Strategy 2

1. Prepare a list of your most important keywords and keyword phrases—the ones your target market will search on if they are looking for a site like yours.

2. Go to the most popular search engines and put in the first keyword or keyword phrase on your list.

3. Copy and paste the top 30 results into a Word, Excel, or other file you will access later.

4. Take the next keyword or keyword phrase on your list from Step 1 and search on it in the most popular search engines.

5. Copy and paste the top 30 results into the Word, Excel, or other file you started in Step 3.

6. Repeat Steps 4 and 5 until you have exhausted all the keywords and keyword phrases on your list. When it is complete, you have your Potential Link Sites list.

7. Now develop a link request letter and keep it open on your desktop so that you can copy and paste it into an e-mail when you find a site that you'd like to have a link from.

8. Next, visit each of the potential link sites to determine whether the site is appropriate for you to be linked from. If the site is appropriate, then send your link request. If the site is not appropriate for whatever reason, delete it from your list.

9. Follow through and follow up. Follow through and provide an appropriate link to those who have agreed to a reciprocal link. Follow up to make sure that they have provided the link to your site as promised, that the link works, and that it is pointing to the correct page on your site.

Second-generation link strategies also incorporated finding and getting linked from meta-indexes or directories relating to your product, service, or geographic area. Web rings were, and still are, good resources for finding appropriate link sites. Some second-generation link strategies included getting linked from link farms or free-for-all sites that were designed specifically to increase link popularity scores. This strategy should **not** be used as the search engines really don't like sites that try to manipulate their ranking. Most of the search engines today penalize sites that are linked from such sites.

As the search engines' ranking criteria became more and more sophisticated, so have the link strategies employed to score high become more and more sophisticated. Many sites incorporate affiliate programs, which certainly send targeted traffic but also help to improve link popularity and link relevancy scores. Some search engines have an element in their ranking formula that looks for the keyword or keyword phrase in the text around the link pointing to a site. Savvy affiliate marketers ensure that their most popular keywords are incorporated in the text around the link to their sites by providing the appropriate information to their affiliates.

Others, when arranging reciprocal links, provide the graphics and HTML coding for the link to their site and make sure to incorporate their most important keywords in the text around the link to their sites.

Still others provide a Link to Us page as shown in Figure 3.1, which again provides the graphics and HTML coding for the link. Of course, they make sure to get the appropriate keywords in the text around the link. You want to change the specific text around the link that you provide on a regular basis as the search engines are always looking for manipulation, and if every link to your site has the exact same text around the link, it will definitely smell of manipulation.

On these Link to Us pages, businesses often provide an incentive for people to take their desired action: "Link to us and be included in a drawing for an

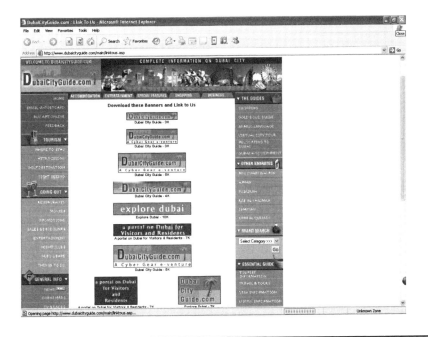

Figure 3.1. This Dubai City Guide provides a variety of types of banners as well as the HTML code to make it easy for any Web site visitor to provide a link to their site.

appropriate prize." You might go a step further and say that the drawing is done monthly and they get a ballot for every page on their site that provides the link.

The programmers at the search engine organizations are very smart, and they don't like sites that try to manipulate or outsmart their formulas. I would suggest that if you employ any of these latest strategies, you change the link details and the accompanying text around the link you provide on a regular basis.

Quality matters when it comes to links. Links from sites that have a significant amount of traffic are more valuable than links from little-known sites. Links from sites that have a high Google Page Rank score are more valuable than links from those with a low Google Page Rank score.

Internet Advertising

The first advertisements on the World Wide Web began in 1994. These ads were always placed at the top of a Web page and were always 60 pixels high and 468 pixels wide and were known as banner ads. Whenever anyone thought about Internet marketing back in those early days, the first thing that came to mind was banner advertising. Back in those days, advertisers managed their own banner advertising campaigns and sites sold their own advertising space.

The second generation came along very quickly. Online advertising agencies started to crop up, managing the banner advertising space for very heavily trafficked sites. If you wanted to advertise on a specific site, you worked with their online agency. To advertise with a number of heavily trafficked sites, you ended up dealing with two or three or four advertising agencies.

Almost as soon as banner advertising became mainstream, it started to decline in effectiveness. Click-through rates dropped through the floor, technology to strip out unwanted ads became very popular, and soon there was all kinds of available advertising space at dirt prices and few takers. Banner advertising was okay for branding, but terrible on generating traffic to your site.

Advertisers used many techniques to try to change things. Various sizes and placement techniques were tried. Animated banner ads saw a little increase in click-throughs. Drop-down menu banner ads were somewhat effective. Many techniques were employed, but with the exception of a few key areas, banner advertising continued to be viewed as generally ineffective.

Targeted advertising on niche content sites was and still is very effective. For example, a meta-index or directory related to ski hills in Vermont would be a very effective site for a ski hill in Vermont to place a banner ad. Keyword banner advertising and geo-targeted banner advertising were still very effective.

The third generation of online advertising is seeing a resurgence. We are seeing a growth in popularity of high-impact rich media ads. The size and placement of ads has changed significantly. The major search engines have very effective keyword advertising programs that are continually being enhanced in terms of targeting. The demand by marketers for greater accountability in the return on investment they get for their ad dollars spent is being met. The results are encouraging them to invest more in this medium. Effective techniques are available for consumers who demand greater control over their media and marketing experiences.

Rich Media Advertising

"Rich media" is a term used to describe a wide variety of media experiences that offer an enhanced interactive experience. Rich media would include things like streaming audio, streaming video, applets that allow user interaction, and special effects.

There are a number of programming technologies that are used to deliver this rich media functionality, and these are continually releasing new features and bells and whistles in keeping with the explosive growth of this medium. DHTML, Java, Javascript, and Flash would be among the most popular rich media programming technologies.

Rich media is appealing to advertisers for a number of reasons. Brand recognition and message association can be achieved very effectively by using audio, video, and animation. Marketing content can be embedded in entertaining content and educational content for those consumers who don't want advertising; hence, the significant growth in "advertainment" and "edutainment."

Marketers totally understand that consumers want to be in control and they do not want to be marketed to. Marketers understand that marketing should be so appealing that consumers want it and invite it into their lives and devices.

Nielsen/NetRatings AdRelevance reports that rich media has risen steadily and significantly over the last five years. The rich media advertising is certainly more appealing to the consumer—more entertaining, more informative, more relevant, and more timely.

Size and Placement

Marketers have long since realized that site visitors have become oblivious to the static 60 pixel high by 468 pixel wide ad at the top of the page. Sites are focusing on a major reduction of clutter on their sites. The trend has been away from the smaller banner and half-button ads and a shift to leader boards, skyscrapers, and large rectangles—all incorporating rich media.

This shift works well for consumers and for advertisers. The consumers are enjoying less clutter. The marketers are seeing higher brand impact.

Search Advertising

Search advertising dates back almost as far as the search engines themselves. Way back in 1995, InfoSeek provided keyword banner advertising—you chose which keywords you were interested in, and when those words were searched on, your banner ad appeared at the top of the search results page.

In 1998, GoTo.com appeared. GoTo.com was the first to provide Internet marketers the opportunity to do text advertising on search engines. GoTo subsequently changed its name to Overture and Overture was bought by Yahoo!

Today Google AdWords and Yahoo! Search Marketing are the main players in search advertising. Advertising with both of these will give you a reach of over 90 percent of the Internet search audience. Yahoo! Search Marketing and Google AdWords sell text-based keyword targeted ads through their own search engines as well as through a network of other search engines.

At the time this book was written, Yahoo! Search Marketing provided keyword targeted ads to Yahoo!, MSN, AltaVista, CNN, AlltheWeb, Sympatico.ca; ISPs Juno and NetZero; meta-search sites like Dogpile, Webcrawler, and Web Crawler; Microsoft Internet Explorer; and tons of content sites including Advertising.com, Coolsavings.com, ESPN, National Geographic, Wall Street Journal, Knight Ridder, Consumer Review Network, and many more.

Google provides targeted keyword ads to AOL, Lycos, AskJeeves, Netscape, Earthlink, CompuServe, Shopping.com, AT&T Worldnet, About.com, The New York Times, Business.com, HGTV, and other heavily trafficked sites.

Search advertising is very straightforward—advertisers bid on specific keywords or keyword phrases to impact their position of the text ads on search results pages, their ad appears when someone does a search on the chosen keywords or keyword phrases, and if (but only if) someone actually clicks on their ad and is delivered to their site, the advertiser pays.

Most major search engines provide the opportunity, either themselves or through a network they belong to, to "pay to play"—that is, you can pay to have a listing appear on the search results page anytime a search is done on a specific keyword or keyword phrase. These paid listings usually appear separately from the organic results—sometimes these sponsored listings appear at the top of the page, sometimes they appear as a sidebar, and sometimes they appear at the bottom of the page.

There are many terms used—paid placement, sponsored listings, pay to play, pay for placement, CPC listings referring to cost per click, and PPC listings referring to pay per click.

Since 85 percent of Internet users, when doing research or looking for something, use the search engines, there are many benefits to this type of advertising:

- Your site will usually appear on page 1 of the search results for your most appropriate keywords if your bid is high enough, albeit in a separate section from the organic results.

- With this type of advertising, you pay for the ad only when someone is actually delivered to your site.

- You get very targeted Web site visitors when they are looking for your type of products or services.

- This type of advertising is fantastic for those sites that choose to use Flash or dynamically generated pages that have a difficult time placing high in the organic search results.

- The program is completely flexible in that you can start or stop advertising at any time immediately, you can change the copy for your ad at any time and it goes live immediately, you can change your bid at any time, and you can have multiple bids for the same keyword.

- Your audience expands immediately. By participating in Yahoo! Search Marketing and Google AdWords alone, you'll reach over 90 percent of the Internet search audience.

- This can be a great vehicle for branding.

- Pay per click advertising is very quantifiable—the results can be measured. Results are provided through the search engine, and you can also use your Web traffic analysis software to provide great results and metrics on search advertising campaigns.

- Search engine advertising is nonintrusive. Search engine traffic starts from a voluntary, visitor-driven search.

All the programs are similar but have a few idiosyncrasies. With Google, being the highest bidder doesn't necessarily guarantee top placement. Their positioning is dependent on click-through rates as well as the bid. With Google, you don't always pay what you bid; you pay a penny above the next lowest competitor.

There are many options with each program to choose from to customize your advertising campaign. Things like:

- You can target your ads to specific countries.

- You can target your ads to specific languages.

- You can run multiple ads for the same keyword phrase.

- You can participate in dayparting programs, which enable you to have your ads run only during certain hours of the day.

- You can set a daily, weekly, or monthly maximum for your bids.

The Google AdWords and Yahoo! Search Marketing sites provide a wealth of information on this type of advertising as well as great tools to assist your campaigns.

Today's savvy Internet marketers are playing heavily in search advertising. Some companies have staff take care of this activity, but many choose to outsource this to companies that have lots of experience running these types of campaigns. However you choose to do it, there are several elements that are critical to your success:

- Keyword/keyword phrase selection is critical to search advertising success. Here it's important to do your homework and know what you're doing. This is not a simple process. There are great tools to assist you, like Wordtracker (see Figure 3.2) and WebPosition Gold. A good search advertising strategy researches keywords, the number of times they have been searched through the popular search engines, keyword combinations, conversion rates, ROI (return on investment), and current bids to come up with a final selection of major and minor keyword phrases and top bids for each one.

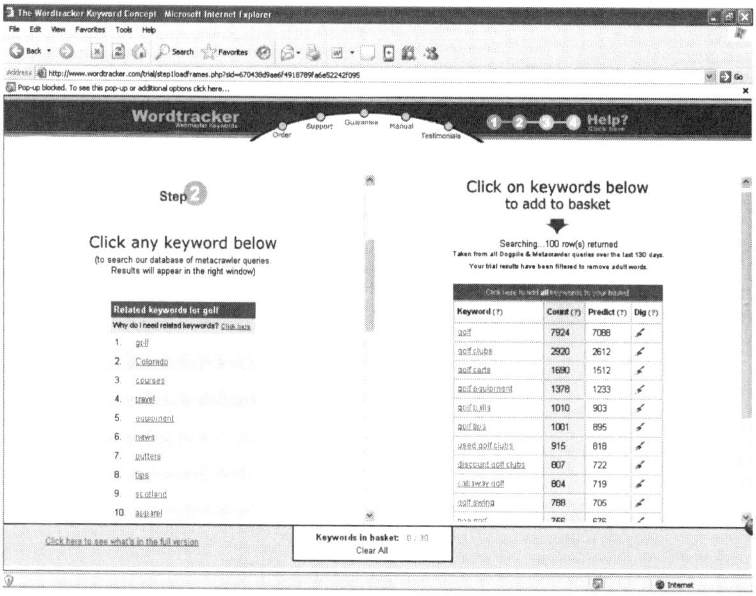

Figure 3.2. Wordtracker provides great tools to help you research and refine your keywords for optimization and PPC.

- Once you have selected the phrases you're going to bid on, the next thing is to develop the ad copy for each one. Copy is critically important! You can edit and change at any time. You can have multiple listings for each using different ad copy; this is generally referred to as A/B creative. You can then monitor to see which copy is pulling more visitors. Copy can be changed to reflect the season or your specials or anything else you think will work. Calls to action are often used—it's amazing how often people do what they are told to do!

- Landing pages are another critical element. For each keyword phrase you bid on, you get to choose which page of your Web site the visitor lands on when he or she clicks on your ad. (See the landing pages in Chapter 5 of this book for details.)

- Measurement is still another critical element in successful campaigns. The reports have to be reviewed and interpreted. Calculations have to be done and interpreted. Modifications to bids, to copy, to keyword selection is an ongoing process to provide top ROI.

Contextual Advertising

One of the latest Internet marketing buzzwords is "contextual advertising." The premise is that it is important to reach your potential customers with your marketing message at the time they are looking for your type of products or services.

What is contextual advertising? In very simplistic terms, it is providing a targeted ad on a Web page based on the content of that Web page.

How does it work? The basic contextual advertising systems or programs scan the text of a Web page looking for keywords and keyword phrases. The contextual advertising system then goes back to its database of ads and looks for a match of those keywords and keyword phrases. It then feeds the appropriate ads to the advertising space on that page. In most cases, the higher the bid by the advertiser, the higher their ad will appear on that page. We are seeing more and more sophisticated programs putting the advertiser in greater control.

Contextual ads can take several forms:

- A skyscraper ad space on the right or left-hand side of the page that holds multiple ads (see Figure 3.3)

- Separate ads that appear in designated advertising spaces on the Web page

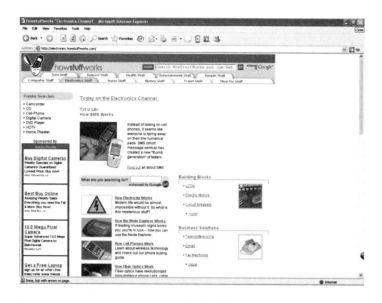

Figure 3.3. On this page related to electronics on the How Stuff Works site are ads related to digital cameras on the left in the blue skyscrapers ads powered by Google.

- Pop-ups.

The benefits to the advertisers are many:

- Your ad is placed in front of potential customers when they are interested in your types of products or services.

- This type of advertising generally costs less than search advertising.

- You pay only when a potential customer is delivered to your site if you purchase this type of advertising on a cost-per-click basis.

- Branding is reinforced every time your listing is viewed.

On the downside:

- Competitors' ads may appear in the same space.

- Sites that you may not want to be associated with can appear in the same space.

- Mismatches do occur.

How do you participate? Most people are familiar with the contextual advertising programs offered by the major search engines—Google's AdSense and Yahoo! Search Marketing's Content Match. Other prominent contextual advertising networks include Kanoodle's Context Target, IndustryBrains, AdSonar, and ContextWeb, to name a few. Blogger.com is a major network for contextual ads for blogs. To find a more complete list, check out the Resource section at susansweeney.com.

Although contextual advertising and search advertising have many similarities (use the same pay-per-click pricing, targeted, based on keywords), contextual advertising is different from search advertising. Contextual advertising has a significantly lower conversion rate than search advertising primarily due to the fact that when someone is searching for something, he or she is definitely looking for that item and is likely more interested in purchasing; the searcher is considered a "shopper." If someone is reading an article on something and clicks through on an ad he or she finds interesting, the reader may or may not be in the purchasing mode; the searcher is considered a "browser." You will always convert more shoppers than browsers.

As with search advertising, when you are doing contextual advertising it is important to manage your campaigns. Plan your budget, diligently choose appropriate keywords, determine the appropriate bids for each of your keywords, and monitor and measure your results.

Behavioral Advertising

What is behavioral targeting? Well, quite simply, it is advertising to Web users based on their previous behavior or activity on the Web. It is the process of identifying potential customers based on the searches they have done, sites they have visited, and specific actions they have taken, and then serving them an appropriate ad at the optimal time.

The more you know about present and potential customers, the better you are able to market to them. Behavioral targeting technologies monitor and track the sites visited, the content read, and the actions taken by individuals on the Web. This is done anonymously—meaning they don't collect personally identifiable information like name, address, e-mail address, or telephone number.

It is done by way of cookies that are installed on the surfer's computer as he or she views ads from online advertising networks. The surfer's actions are then tracked and stored in a database—things like Web sites visited, how long he or she stayed on specific content pages, etc. The databased information is then analyzed and used to predict future behavior based on past experience of others in the database. Behavioral ad networks then serve targeted advertising to those individuals whenever they visit a site that is served ads by their network.

Behavioral targeting can be implemented several ways. It can be implemented through a Web site, through an advertising network, or on your computer through adware.

Behavioral advertising uses leading-edge, real-time technologies. It is hot because it is targeted and it works. According to a recent Ponemon study, behavioral targeted advertising is projected to increase by 65 percent in 2006.

Some of the leading players with behavioral advertising right now are TACODA, 24/7 Media, AlmondNet, Drive PM, Accipiter, and Revenue Science—these are the people who are actually working with the publishers to provide behavioral targeting.

Measurement and Accountability

Companies have been demanding more and more accountability before they move more and more of their marketing budgets to advertising online. The third-generation advertising measurement metrics do not disappoint them. Ask and ye shall receive. Back in the olden days, statistics like impressions and click-throughs were acceptable. Today savvy marketers are provided with anything and everything their heart desires in terms of advertising measurement. Hence, we are seeing more mainstream ad dollars continue to shift rapidly online.

Common third-generation metrics that measure the effectiveness of online advertising campaigns include things like:

- Interaction times—time spent and brand interaction

- Post-click conversions

- Cost per conversion

- View-through conversions

- Average frequency of exposures

- Frequency-to-conversion ratio

- Share of voice

- Brand lift

- Offline sales lift or impact

- Detailed rich media interactions

- Total display time for an ad on a user's page

- Total time spent exploring features of an ad

- Interactions the reader makes with the mouse over the ad

- Unique reach of ads delivered

- Mega-panel behavioral tracking

- Web page eye tracking

- Keyword search usage

- View-through rate (i.e., delayed visits to advertiser's site, visits without a direct ad click-through)

- Ad exposure time (rich media)

- Ad interaction rate (rich media)

- Cross-media mix modeling

- Cross-media mix econometric modeling.

Affiliate Marketing

Affiliate marketing started very early in the game. One of the first, Amazon.com, introduced its affiliate program in 1996. Today Amazon has over 1 million affiliates worldwide promoting their products and sending Amazon interested, warm, potential customers. The program today works basically the same as it did then:

1. A person, company, or organization joins Amazon's affiliate program and becomes an Associate.

2. The Associate sends traffic to Amazon.com through specially formatted links that allow Amazon to track sales and other actions.

3. Associates earn referral fees on all sales made as a result of their links.

In the beginning, affiliate programs had fairly sophisticated technology but relatively unsophisticated implementation; referrals were generally made through banner ad type links. The cost to implement these affiliate programs was a significant investment for a business. The attitude of merchants was the more affiliates the better.

Affiliate marketing is ideal for merchants in that fees are only paid on performance. Fees can be set as a fixed amount or as a percentage. Payment can be made on cost-per-click, cost-per-sale, cost-per-action, or cost-per-lead basis. Most often the referral fee is paid on the sale as a percentage of the sale; however, there are many cost-per-action campaigns in existence. A popular example of the cost-per-action is a set fee for each person the affiliate encourages to join a merchant's e-club or e-specials permission-based marketing list.

Today things are very different in the affiliate marketing world. No longer are the links provided through banner ad type buttons on the affiliate's site. Today affiliate marketing can be done through signature files, e-mails, autoresponder replies, help files, software products, games, viral marketing, java applets, demos, ftp sites, active-x controls, Flash, e-zine articles, blogs, RSS feeds, and e-books.

No longer is the focus on mass affiliation. Instead, the focus is on quality rather than quantity. Today, affiliate managers would rather focus on the active affiliates providing them with much more personalized service. These affiliate managers have to monitor and police affiliates to make sure they are in compliance with the company's policies and procedures, are in compliance with spam policies and legislation, and are not doing anything to damage the merchant's reputation.

Program management is another area that has changed quite dramatically. In the olden days, a merchant would provide access to banners through its extranet, and there was little communication between the merchant and the affiliates. Today program management is critical to the success of an affiliate marketing program. Merchants have a person or a team responsible for "feeding" the affiliates new material, new techniques, and new ideas to increase their business.

Today we have an increasing number of smart Internet marketers who are in it for the money. They are good at what they do, enjoy doing it, and are looking for great affiliate marketing programs with great products, a great compensation program, and great affiliate managers providing them with great tools and service to do what they do best.

Successful affiliate networks know that the most important thing is communication with their affiliates. Many merchants are providing significant training resources to their affiliates through their extranet. Affiliates already have access to a plethora of reports available through the extranet in real time to be able to track their own performance. They can track and measure their performance immediately after they run a campaign. They can see what's working and what's not.

Today management knows that affiliates send the warm traffic, but it is their responsibility to convert. Much emphasis is placed on the elements on the landing page, the ad copy, and the techniques used to convert that warm visitor into a paying customer.

On the one hand, the benefits of having an affiliate program are significant:

- Affiliates send targeted, prequalified potential customers to the merchant's Web site.

- Every affiliate link helps the merchant with search engine optimization by increasing their link popularity score and very often their link relevancy score as well.

The issues facing online merchants and the affiliate also are many:

- Privacy and security laws

- Adware and spyware litigation and legislation

- CAN-SPAM in the United States, PIPEDA in Canada, and other legislation around the world

- FTC advertising rules and regulations

- Contracts, terms, and conditions of affiliate programs

- Intellectual property issues

- Fraudulent business practices.

We are still in the infancy stages of affiliate marketing. These next few years will see significant online sales growth through 3G, Wi-Fi, and other technology. With that comes an even greater opportunity for affiliate marketing. We will continue to see technology enhancements as well as enhancements on the human side of things from the affiliate manager to the affiliates. Stay tuned.

RSS

What is RSS? "RSS" is an acronym for Really Simple Syndication. RSS is a format for syndicating news and other content that can be broken down into discrete items. Once information is in RSS format on a site, an RSS reader can check the feed for updates and react to the updates in a predefined way.

How does this work? The technology behind RSS enables you to subscribe to Web sites that have provided RSS feeds (see Figure 3.4). These sites typically add new content on a regular basis.

To use RSS, you need an RSS news reader or news aggregator that enables you to access and display the RSS content either on your computer or

Figure 3.4. Wired News provides one page where you can subscribe to its newsletter, download Wired News to your handheld, or subscribe to the RSS feed to download the latest Wired headlines to your site.

directly on your Web site. There are many different RSS readers or news aggregators available for free. You do the research, find the one you want to use, download it, and install it. The news aggregator helps you keep up with all your favorite resources by checking their RSS feeds and displaying the new or recent items from each of them. They usually give you only a descriptive line or two and a link to the full article.

Alternatively, you can use a Web-based service that works with your browser. After you run through your initial setup, you subscribe to any RSS service you want to access on a regular basis.

The content that you are provided with usually includes a headline, a description, and a link to the Web page that provides all the details. The RSS readers automatically retrieve updates from sites that you have subscribed to, providing you with up-to-the-minute content as it is published.

There are many ways savvy Internet marketers are using RSS to communicate with their target markets on an ongoing basis:

- Specials, promotions, coupons, and packages feeds—Everyone wants a deal or a bargain. Provide your own through an RSS feed or work with other sites that have the same target market to promote your products or services. We're getting into personalized feeds where a subscriber can state preferences: "I want travel and pet coupons but don't want financial services coupons." There are all kinds of these RSS feeds—airlines feeding out latest deals, travel agencies with last-minute deals, software companies with latest releases and upgrades. The opportunities here are plentiful. Partnering with other sites that appeal to your target market, have significant traffic, and are selling noncompeting products/services provides a wide distribution of your content.

- Press releases via RSS—Companies are providing their press releases and company announcements via RSS feeds. Many of the major press release distribution services/wire services provide media with feeds. With press release distribution, you can either have your own feed or work with others that have your target market as their subscribers.

- Affiliate marketing—RSS feeds are ideal for affiliate marketers. These feeds can be used in a number of different ways. Specials, coupons, and product information can be incorporated into affiliate Web sites, complete with the affiliate's unique identifier tags. Affiliate marketers can also use this technology to keep their affiliates current, motivated, and armed with the latest product information, promotions, articles, and ads.

- Classifieds—People are subscribing to receive the latest classifieds that are of interest. Subscribers can sign up to receive the ads related to jobs from certain companies or certain industries or certain types of positions. You might be looking for a house in a specific area and sign up to receive real estate ads for open houses or listings in defined areas. You might be looking for a specific make or model of automobile and sign up to receive classifieds that fit the profile.

- Branded content—Brand your content by providing relevant, interesting information to sites that speak to your target market. If your business is a golf course, you might have the golf pro develop golf tips to be provided to other golf-related sites. I could develop content on Internet marketing tips, tools, techniques, and resources that could be provided to Internet marketing sites or sites that want to provide Internet marketing information to their visitors. Whenever you brand your content, make sure that you get your profile in the resource box and a link back to the appropriate section of your Web site.

There are many, many opportunities to use RSS feeds in an Internet marketing capacity. As with everything in Internet marketing, you need to develop content after giving consideration to:

- Your objectives with this Internet marketing technique

- Your target market(s) for this technique

- The specific products and services you want to promote with this technique

- You will want to give consideration to the terms of use for your content. Do you want to limit the content to noncommercial use on others' sites or is it okay if they use it for commercial purposes?

Always make sure that you have mandatory source identification. When others use your content and want to publish or distribute it, you will want a resource box identifying you as the provider and, more importantly, a link to your Web site.

For the content that will bring you the most business, you want to publish it on a Tuesday, Wednesday, or Thursday. Tuesday is the most active day for RSS readership. The time of day is important as well. Morning scanners view the most content, whereas the midnight cowboys tend to have a higher click-through rate.

Blogging

A blog is a chronological publication or online journal of postings to a Web site. Often these blogs look like a running diary. Blogs are also called Web logs or Weblogs, but most often the term "blog" is used so as not to cause confusion with the reference of Web logs to the server's log files. There are millions of these online journals, growing at a rate of tens of thousands per day, linking together to form a vast network.

Blogs have been around for a while, but really have come into the mainstream with the introduction of automated publishing systems like Blogger at *http://www.blogger.com* that made it really easy for Web site owners to add this type of content. Google acquired Blogger.com in 2003.

There are all kinds of sites like Bloglines (see Figure 3.5) that provide you with Web based tools to create your own blog, subscribe to others, and search for blogs that are of interest.

Consumers' desire to have more control over "real" information as opposed to what the media wants them to have has grown significantly over the last few years. Blogs often are seen to be unbiased consumer-generated content and thus have grown in popularity over that same time period. The technology enables anyone to broadcast information, pictures, and videos worldwide in a

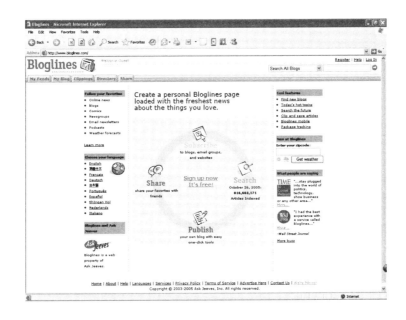

Figure 3.5. Bloglines is a Web-based personal news aggregator that can be used in place of a desktop aggregator.

matter of minutes. No more waiting for video or pictures on CNN of the latest hurricane or disaster. Bloggers can have the content up instantaneously, others link to it, and it is all over the Web in a matter of minutes.

Blogs tend to focus on a niche, and every niche is covered. There are blogs related to the music industry, cheat sheets for online games, children's products, travel in Russia, and everything in between. Business-to-business blogs are one of the fastest-growing segments. There may be blogs out there talking about your business, your products, your customer service, or your share value. Your employees may have blogs providing the world with an inside view of the company.

Blogs are informal—great for relationship building. Blogs are easy to maintain. Blogs are informative. The blog can be maintained by you yourself, or you can allow your Web site visitors to participate. This can be a great feature as long as your customers are going to post positive comments. They are usually updated daily; this may be a problem if you don't have THAT much news. On the other hand, if you don't have much Web site traffic, why do this? As with everything related to Internet marketing, always go back to review your objectives, your target markets, and your products and services to determine if this is an appropriate Internet marketing technique for you and your business.

Many companies are starting to take blogging as a serious form of marketing and information distribution. They know that potential customers are on the Internet looking for the latest information on their types of products or services. They are looking for recommendations. They are looking for the best deal. They are looking for the latest.

Small and large companies alike are delving into blogs as a vehicle to get the word out about their products and services. You can set up a free account at Blogger.com or any of the other free services and you can start broadcasting in minutes. Back in the olden days, if a company wanted to get some information out, it would have to develop press releases, get them approved by the powers that be in their PR department, distribute these releases, and follow up with the editors to try to get some coverage. There was a cost to all of this, and your story may or may not get picked up. Today anyone can become a blog publisher in about 10 minutes and start providing their information to the world.

Microsoft has set up a video blog to speak to the online developer community.

Blogs have a number of interesting Internet marketing applications:

- Paid advertising on other people's blogs. You are looking for a blog that is being read by your target market when they are discussing your types of products or services. Be careful here, as audiences can be very touchy if they feel they are being marketed to through the blog. Advertising is much more effective in blogs if they are more of an advertorial—where the ad fits the blog topic so well that it seems to be part of the conversation rather than an advertisement.

- Sponsorship opportunities on other peoples blogs. Again, you are looking for a good fit between the blog's visitors and your target market.

- Corporate owned and operated blogs

- Link strategies. Being linked from blogs will help a site improve from a search engine optimization standpoint. The link will increase the link popularity score and may assist in link relevancy score as well.

Many businesses have developed corporate policies and procedures around blogs. Employees need to know if they are allowed to mention your corporation in their blogs. They should be provided with what is acceptable and what isn't, and if they are allowed to include any corporate reference in their blog.

Many businesses have assigned a person in their marketing department the responsibility of monitoring the blogs for mention of the company. They have policies and procedures in place for their reaction when they find their company mentioned. If it's good news, they want to capitalize on the mention by getting as many links to it as possible and getting the "right" people to see it. If it's bad news, they need to have procedures in place to minimize the damage.

Blogs provide a plethora of information related to target market research. You can find out what present and potential customers think about your products or services, your advertising campaigns, your advertising slogans, or their preferences related to style, color, or features.

We're in the initial stages of blogging, but we're already seeing offshoots.

- Moblogging—the posting to a blog in real time from a camera phone, PDA, or other handheld device.

- Video blogging—bloggers can post video diaries online.

- Flogs or fake blogs—Talk about guerilla marketing! Corporations have employees using an alias set up a blog to tout the company's products, services, or happenings.

Podcasting/Videocasting

Podcasting is a relatively recent addition to Internet marketing. What is podcasting? The term is a combination of two terms—"broadcasting" and "iPod"—the latter referring to Apple's portable digital audio player, although any MP3 player can play the content.

Podcasting is basically a method of publishing audio content via the Internet, allowing users to subscribe to a feed of new files—usually MP3s. Podcasting became very popular in late 2004.

You can browse the Internet to find podcasts that are of interest (see Figure 3.6); you can sample and subscribe to those that you're interested in and then sync them to your MP3 player to be able to listen to them anywhere, anytime. Once you subscribe to a podcast, your device will automatically check for updates and download new programs to your computer. When you sync your device, all your podcasts are delivered to that device.

Now you can listen to your favorite talk show while jogging. You can listen to the 6 a.m. news at 10:27. You can listen to Susan Sweeney's Internet Marketing training programs while sitting by the pool. You can listen to movie reviews while standing in line at the theatre.

Figure 3.6. Podcast Net is a directory of podcasts.

Podcasting can be distributed by RSS. As you saw in the RSS section of this chapter, RSS allows subscribers to view Web site content coming from source Web sites. Similarly, podcasts allow you to listen to audio content coming from source Web sites.

Podcasts have many benefits to subscribers:

1. They get great content on subjects that interest them. There are podcasts on every topic imaginable—everything from Internet marketing to Thai cooking. There are many podcast directories popping up all over the Web to make it easy to find the content you are looking for. From a marketing perspective, you want to see if there is an opportunity to develop your own podcasts to provide to your target market. You also want to look at wide distribution or even syndication of your podcasts for maximum exposure.

2. The technology puts the subscribers in control. They can access what they want and listen to it when they want, wherever they are; no more having to be in front of a computer or within radio frequency range. The listener can be on a plane, exercising, or in a hot tub.

3. Content, at this stage, is often still free to the subscriber. However, this may change as content providers grow their subscriber database and become known for their great content. Others may never charge a fee and will use this as an advertising mechanism, being careful to appropriately incorporate their product information into the podcast content.

4. Podcast content is very often niched. This is of great interest to the podcast user, but also provides a great, highly targeted opportunity for the podcast marketer.

Podcast marketers will have to be very sensitive to advertising in this medium to the target market as users are looking for control and ad avoidance. Too much blatant advertising and they will unsubscribe. Today we are seeing very short, and I mean *very* short (like 15-second), audio ads embedded into the content. It is far better for savvy Internet marketers to figure out how to include your message as part of the content than as an ad. Key marketing opportunities will be in the noninterruptive marketing models like content integration and sponsorship.

Although for most, podcasting is a relatively new marketing technology, we will see videocasting hot on its heels. Videocasting will be a combination of audio and video that will be downloaded by subscribers to be viewed on their 3G phones, personal video players, and PCs.

Mobile Marketing

With mobile devices we can do all kinds of things—check our flight schedule, transfer money from one account to another, pay our credit card bill, make a hotel reservation, check our investment portfolio, take and send a picture, watch a video, check the score of the baseball game, check the weather in Topeka. With the new 3G devices we can do even more, faster.

The mobile marketplace is significant. There are over 1.8 billion people out there with a mobile device capable of voice, text, image, and Internet communication. This number is increasing at a rapid pace as less-developed countries like China and India are going straight to wireless for their phones.

We are seeing swift and wide acceptance with over 350 billion text messages exchanged over the world's mobile networks each month. The Yankee Group tells us that over 15 percent of these messages are classified as commercial or marketing messages, telling me that there are 52.5 billion marketing messages currently being exchanged monthly.

Mobile marketing is a marketer's dream. It allows direct, personal communication in real time with the opportunity for immediate, direct response. Mobile marketing can be used to:

- Improve customer loyalty

- Increase brand awareness

- Build a customer profile in your permission-based opt-in database

- Send potential customers to your bricks-and-mortar locations

- Increase sales.

There are a number of mobile marketing opportunities—instant messaging, location-based services, profile-specific advertising, subscribed content, SMS (short messaging service), MMS (multimedia messaging service), and mobile blogging.

- Instant messaging—Wireless providers are including instant messaging as part of their services. The second annual AOL Instant Messaging Survey showed that a whopping 59 percent of Internet users use instant messaging on a regular basis, 29 percent send more instant messages than e-mail, and 20 percent of instant messaging users send mobile instant messages or SMS text messages through a mobile personal device. The survey provided stats to indicate that it's not just teenagers getting in on this phenomenon—instant messaging is being used by 90 percent of online 13- to 21-year-olds, 71 percent of 22- to 34-year-olds, 55 percent of 34- to 54-year-olds, and an amazing 48 percent of those over 55.

- Location-based services—As the name would suggest, location-based services use location as a key element in providing relevant information to users. There are many mobile marketing applications for location-based services. You are hosting a meeting in another city and want to find the closest Staples shop to e-mail your print job to. Your flight has been cancelled and you want to find the closest hotel. It's your anniversary and you have to find the flower shop closest to your wife's office. You are in a strange city and want to find the closest Thai restaurant with directions on how to get from where you are to there with detailed instructions. With the convergence of so many technologies, you can even have your mobile device talk to you to tell you how to get there.

Technology is being developed to be able to identify the specific geographic location, within 5 to 10 yards, of the telephone. This allows the opportunity to send highly targeted location-based advertising to the device. This opens up a whole new range of opportunities for marketers. We've been hearing for years about the scenario where you will be walking by Starbucks when your cell phone will vibrate. When you review your mobile device screen, you see that there's a two-for-one special for Starbucks that has been sent to you.

Another technology we understand is coming is the bar code reader attachment for the telephone. Every item for sale in the world has a bar code. You'll be able to scan an item and, using your mobile device, go to the Internet to find where the best deal is on that particular item within whatever radius you define.

Location-based services will change the way we do lots of things. In speaking about this at conferences, I jokingly recommend that if the boss has provided you with a cell phone or mobile device and you're going golfing on Friday afternoon, leave the boss's device at the office and set it to call forward to your own device. If you're looking for brownie points, leave it there for the weekend.

- Profile-specific advertising—Because each phone has a unique identi-fier in the phone number, it is possible to build the profile of the owner of each device. Once you have a profile, it is then possible to send very targeted advertising messages to that profile. This type of advertising needs to be carefully deployed to ensure that it is not considered intru-sive, spam, or unsolicited.

- Subscribed content—Marketers look for permission-based mobile marketing opportunities. In April, Teen People announced that it will send weekly updates and breaking news along with targeted advertise-ments and promotions to subscribers' mobile phones.

- SMS (short messaging service)—SMS allows text messages of up to 160 alpha-numeric characters (no images or graphics) to be sent and received on your mobile phone. The message can also be sent to your mobile phone from the Internet using an SMS gateway Web site. If the phone is turned off or is out of range, the message is stored on the network and is delivered the next time you power on.

A recent e-Marketer study reports that 39 percent of mobile users in Asia have received SMS messages from advertisers, 36 percent in Europe, and only 8 percent in the United States.

Early campaigns have mainly been contest-oriented—text to win or tied in with major events. Coke ran an SMS campaign in China which it deemed to be successful. The ad campaign ran for a little over a month. Participants had to guess the highest daily temperature in Beijing and enter the contest via an SMS. Coke said that more than 4 million messages were exchanged in the 35-day duration of the "Coke Cool Summer" interactive contest. The SMS contest was promoted through a television ad offering free downloads of the Coke jingle and McDonald's coupons. The campaign was user-initiated and was not intrusive.

We have recently seen the SMS voting for your favorite "American Idol" television program. It was very interesting to see that over one-third of the voters were first-time SMSers; this was their introduction to SMS. We are seeing all kinds of SMS promotions kicking in.

- MMS (multimedia messaging service)—MMS is an enhanced trans-mission service enabling color images, video clips, text, and sound files to be sent and received by cell phones. The 3G phones are all equipped with MMS capability.

MMS brings a whole new dimension to mobile marketing by enabling color pictures, audio, and video into the marketing message. The marketing opportunities are endless for this technology. The benefits for marketers abound—immediate contact, immediate response, multimedia capability engaging a number of the senses. Combine this with the ability to know where your subscriber is physically within 5 to 10 yards as well as having a profile of the subscriber—a marketer's dream.

Some examples of the ways in which MMS is already being used:

- Film news—Subscribers receive the up-to-the-second news on what's going on in Hollywood and the latest film news.

- Voting—Subscribers can vote for all kinds of things: their American Idol, who should receive the Best Leading Lady award, who should replace Regis, which of your new logos they like the best. Voting can be simple ("what's your favorite color?") or advanced with multiple-choice and open-ended questions.

- Games—Subscribers could have to take a quiz to answer questions about your company, your products or services, your history, your features, your benefits, anything you want.

- Contest entry—Subscribers can enter to win your contest.

- Instant win—Subscribers can find out if they are a winner immediately.

- Coupons—Subscribers can receive coupons via MMS. They appear on the screen with the expiry time. Show the coupon for the deal. This will drive people to your business. This can be coupled with location-based services.

• mBlogging or mobile blogging—MMS color picture, text, video, and audio can be instantly added to a blog in a matter of seconds. Baseball fans can post their pictures of the game and details of what's happening as it's happening. Picture this—you are the owner of a spa and there is a heavily trafficked spa blog that you'd like to get some profile on. You invite the owner of the blog to your spa and within seconds through mblogging, pictures of your spa can be incorporated into the blog; audio of the blog owner's interview with you can be incorporated as well as a great video of your facilities.

We are in the infancy stages of mobile marketing, and this can take one of two twists. On the one hand, mobile marketing may be treated with the utmost respect for privacy and everything will be permission-based with the device owners subscribing to the services they are interested in, providing their priorities and preferences (how often they want to receive information, when they want to receive it, where they want to receive it), and mobile marketing will be a good thing, much appreciated by the consumer. On the other hand, things could spiral out of control very quickly with unsolicited messages and constant advertising popping up, interrupting your calls and use of the mobile device by people trying to sell you products you don't need, don't want, and didn't ask for.

Viral Marketing

Viral marketing is any online marketing technique that encourages Web site visitors or digital content recipients to pass on a marketing message to others, creating an exponential increase in the message's exposure. Marketers hope their marketing message spreads like a virus—one minute it's nowhere and the next minute it's all over the place.

One of the first examples of viral marketing in the early days was introduced by Amazon. When you were reviewing the details of a specific book on Amazon's site, you were given the opportunity to tell a friend about this book. If you clicked on that option, a pop-up would be provided for you to provide your name and e-mail address, your friend's name and e-mail address, and a short message. Once you completed that information and hit the Send button, the message would be sent. Your friend would receive a message in his or her inbox from you (not Amazon) with the recommendation of the book, a link to it, and your personal message. The advantages to this type of marketing are quite obvious:

1. The message is from someone known to the recipient and is much more likely to be opened and paid attention to.

2. The merchant is given exposure to individuals it had no way of contacting otherwise.

3. Because the message is from a friend, it is basically a third-party recommendation of the specific product from a trusted source.

In the early days, we also started to see other forms of viral marketing—things like "Tell a friend about our site" buttons, postcards on travel-related sites, and various "Tell a friend" and "Send a friend" elements. Some of the more advanced marketers were incorporating product logos, branding elements, or product information into very entertaining film clips that spread around the Web like wildfire.

Successful viral promotions tend to fall into one of three categories:

1. Entertainment—Anything that is funny or amusing tends to be passed on. Jokes, funny videos, songs, games, and anything humorous tend to be passed along.

2. Deals or freebies—Special deals, contests with great prizes, coupons, free offers, and these sorts of things tend to be forwarded to friends. The better the deal, the more it is passed on.

3. Humanitarian—A child is missing, pass this on, online petitions, relief efforts, and fund raisers all tend to be forwarded frequently.

As marketers have gained experience with viral campaigns over the last number of years and have measured the results to see what works and what doesn't, there have been a few subtle changes to viral campaigns that have improved their effectiveness.

Viral campaigns today of the "Tell a friend" variety all are associated with something specific. We know that "Tell a friend about this site" is nowhere as effective as having the viral element tied in with something specific: "Tell a friend about this product" or "Tell a friend about this special."

Providing an incentive increases the uptake on viral marketing. "Tell a friend about our special and receive a ballot in our contest" or "Tell three friends about our golf package to be included in a drawing for this golf bag" will see a higher uptake than a viral marketing promotion with no incentive.

All successful viral campaigns are personalized. The recipient's first name is incorporated throughout the e-mail—in the subject line, in the salutation, and throughout the body. The sender's name is also incorporated into the message as well, to reinforce the recommendation from a trusted source.

The more innovative and interesting, the higher the uptake. On April Fool's Day Workopolis offered all MSN.ca Web site visitors the opportunity to send a fake press release to their friends. There were a number of templates provided to choose from—things like announcements of the sender's new job as CEO, TV news anchor, or supermodel. The viral campaign was a resounding success, far exceeding Workopolis's expectations.

The Mazda Motors UK Women Drivers Parking Video was a great success in that it not only achieved 4.2 million video views, but it also drove (pardon the pun) measurable car sales.

Dreamworks developed a viral marketing site for the horror flick *The Ring 2*. The way the campaign ran was that viewers went to the Web site and entered a friend's e-mail address and cell phone number. The site then sent an e-mail to the friend, inviting him or her to view the movie's trailer online along with a link to it. When the friend clicked on the link and several seconds later is deeply engrossed in viewing the horror flick, his or her cell phone would ring and, upon answering it, he or she heard a whispered "seven days," which just about prompts a heart attack. Dreamworks did this viral campaign in a number of countries, but not in the United States.

With the huge increase in mobile marketing poised to explode over the next year, we can expect viral marketing to integrate into the mix in a much bigger way than it has to this point. We will also see a shift from marketers marketing at people to marketers providing an environment where it is conducive for consumers to market to each other.

Autoresponder Marketing

The first generation of autoresponders was basically Out of Office notifications where you turned the autoresponder on when you were going to be out of the office for a period of time and wanted to let people know this in case they were expecting an immediate response to their e-mail.

The second generation of autoresponders saw them being used for different purposes like sending price lists and e-brochures, but still using very simple technology. A request was sent to a specific e-mail address and the predefined response was immediately returned with the requested information.

Over the last few years, we have seen major changes in the technology being used. The enhanced features have provided many opportunities for marketers and merchants alike.

Today's autoresponders are more sophisticated and are getting better every day; new features and bells and whistles are being added all the time. Autoresponders enable you to provide an immediate response to prospects and customers 24 hours a day, 7 days a week, 365 days a year without the need for human interaction.

In terms of mail list administration, autoresponders have changed dramatically. These programs gather the e-mail addresses of people requesting information and store them in a database. The program adds new names to the database and monitors and eliminates e-mail addresses that no longer work.

Today's autoresponder programs also provide reports about site visitors requesting information, number of new requests, number of unsubscribes, number of nondeliverables, and these types of things.

Tracking reports are also available to provide information on how many people opened the correspondence, how many people followed a specific link to your Web site, how many people downloaded the coupon, or how many people forwarded the message to a friend.

Personalization is also a standard feature of today's autoresponder programs.

Sequential autoresponders enable the first message to go out immediately with a follow-up message scheduled to go several days later and a further follow-up to go several days after that. Market research shows that a prospect needs to be exposed to your message multiple times to become a motivated buyer.

Information marketers are real winners with the enhancements to this technology. We are seeing all kinds of multiple-week courses being delivered through autoresponders. My six-week Secrets of Search Engine Success is delivered through autoresponder technology. When someone purchases this course, the first lesson is received immediately and then a subsequent lesson arrives each week for the duration of the course.

Things like Golf Tip of the Week for golf courses or Featured Destination of the Week for travel agencies or Flaxseed Recipe of the Month for an organic foods merchant are all examples of the types of ways these autoresponders can use this technology to stay in front of the eyes and minds of their target customers.

You can incorporate viral marketing messages to encourage recipients to tell others about the information they are receiving or provide a copy to their friends. Whenever you use viral marketing, make sure you provide the recipient easy access to the opportunity to subscribe to receive the same information.

Autoresponders are easy to set up and require very little maintenance and work.

Permission-Based E-mail Marketing

First-generation e-mail marketing was very basic. Most marketers started out using their e-mail program for this type of communication. Everything was text-based back in the olden days. We couldn't easily segment our database. We couldn't easily personalize our communication. We couldn't track to see what happened once our e-mail was sent. Administration was a real nightmare—manually adding, deleting, and changing e-mail addresses as requests came in.

Fairly early on in the second generation, e-mail was one of the areas that marketers focused on. It was a great way to get in front of your target market on a regular basis to get traffic to your Web site, to increase brand recognition, and to promote your products or services.

Mail list programs were introduced that enable marketers to build their databases. Permission marketing became very important. Mail list software was integrated with your Web site to reduce or eliminate the need for manual administration activities. Personalization in the subject line, salutation, and body of the e-mail became a standard feature. The mail list database was developed so segmentation was easily achieved, allowing you to send strategic communication to select portions of your database.

We saw legislation introduced related to privacy issues, spam, pornography, and commercial e-mails.

As people got sick and tired of receiving spam, we saw wide adoption of spam filters on both the individual recipient and the ISP levels. With that came the need for all marketers to run all outgoing marketing messages through spam checkers.

Today more than 30 billion—yes, with a "b"—e-mails are sent worldwide each and every day. Statistics are all over the place on the amount of spam, but a common number is that 25 percent of all e-mails received are considered spam. The result is tons of filtering on both the ISP and the individual level, dismal metrics, dissatisfied marketers, ticked-off customers, angry ISPs, and government legislators in a quandary over what to do about all this.

Today permission-based e-mail marketers are focused on several things:

- Growing their database of target market prospects significantly in as short a time as possible through permission-based marketing

- Learning as much as they can about every person in their database—actually building a profile of each person through the use of various technologies

- Providing consistently valuable information to the database on a regular basis

- Encouraging people in the database to spread the word.

We cover a great deal of permission-based e-mail marketing in the section on campaign execution in Chapter 5.

VOIP

Voice over Internet Protocol is a technology for the two-way transmission of telephone calls over the Internet, intranets, local area networks, and wide area networks. Calls can be made from PC to PC, PC to phone, or phone to phone.

There are many advantages of VOIP, not the least of which is that you avoid the long-distance charges of the traditional telephone service; VOIP offerings typically are a fixed monthly fee for unlimited long-distance services. VOIP is portable. Wherever you have an Internet connection, your phone number can follow; you're traveling, but when people call your number, they access you no matter where in the world you are.

Other current and future advantages of this technology include:

- Free interoffice calls for offices that have multiple office locations throughout the world.

- Unlimited voicemail boxes with the ability to set up rules to determine which message is played to which caller. The marketing implications here are many. One message could be played to customers, a different message to potential customers, and a different message to be played to suppliers, etc. Because telephone numbers can be identified in your database as to category, this can easily be accomplished.

- See who is calling and bring up their profile before you answer the phone. Customer relationship management (CRM) is key.

- Set your area code to be anywhere you want. Make it easy for customers to call you without having to incur long distance charges even though you are not local.

- Work anywhere. Because your number follows you, you will receive your business calls anywhere you want to. Move your office, but you don't have to change your number.

- On-screen dialing. While you're online, you can click on an Outlook or CRM database contact and the number will be dialed automatically. As voice recognition becomes more prevalent, you'll be able to simply say the name or number and it will be dialed automatically.

- CRM/database integration. Information will flow both ways. When you want to contact someone, you can do so from the database. When you contact someone or he or she contacts you, the details and date of that call will flow back into the CRM system or your database.

- Record calls with the click of a button and store them for future reference. You can attach them to a CRM record.

- Monitoring. See who is currently on the phone, who is in or out of the office, who is calling you, etc.

A significant advantage in the third generation will be that as VOIP becomes more and more prevalent with users, marketers will provide VOIP access through their Web sites so that when you are on a site you can, with the click of a button, be speaking directly with a person in that organization.

VOIP will be integrated everywhere online. When your site appears as the result of a Google search, along with your title, Web address, and short description, will appear a telephone symbol so that the user can instantly access you through the search result.

In 2004 I set up VOIP in my speaking office, our consulting office, and in my homes in Florida, in Nova Scotia, and even at our cottage. I did it myself in under an hour. I set my Florida telephone number with a Nova Scotia area code so that friends and family in Canada don't have to incur long distance when calling me in Florida.

VOIP applications are evolving quickly. For the latest on this and any other Internet marketing technique or technology, check the Resources section of the *http://www.susansweeney.com* Web site.

4

Starting with the Foundation— Your Web Site

You're reading this section of the book, so we can only assume you are considering developing a Web site for your business or you have doubts about what you have now. Before you read any further into this chapter, sit back and ask yourself a question:

For whom do you design your Web site?

When it boils down to it, there are only three real reasons that make sense for developing a Web site for your business, right?

- Make more money

- Spend less money

- Do both more efficiently.

Yup, those are great **benefits** to having a Web site, but you're not designing a Web site for **you**. If you take but one thing away from this section of the book, it should be this—you're designing a Web site for your customers (target market).

Your customers will determine your success. To be successful, you need more customers and you need to keep your customers. You may have repeat customers who are coming to you first to look for a specific item or you may have potential customers who happen to find your site from a search on a related topic. In both cases, it is up to you to give them what they need to make the decision to buy from you.

Your customers expect you to have a Web site, and they expect it to answer all their questions and fulfill all their needs. If it does not, they will find a competitor of yours who can.

In this chapter we cover a number of topics including:

- Twenty reasons you need a Web site for your business

- Know the purpose of your Web site

- The Q2C Model—the genetics of a great Web site

- Eight strategic steps to developing a successful Web site

- Making the right choices.

We're not going to teach you how to develop a Web site; there are plenty of Web site development books out there for that. On our last look, Amazon.com had some 1,700+ books on topics relating to Web site development.

When you finish reading this section, we want you to walk away with a good understanding of the business logic behind building a great Web site and how it all comes together, so that you can make the right choices when planning your Web site. Remember, you're designing your Web site for your customers, so make the investment to do it right and in the end your business will reap the benefits!

Twenty Reasons You Need a Web Site for Your Business

We are a little shocked that we even need to address this topic at this day and age, yet we still encounter businesses firm in their belief that they do not need a Web site. A Web site should be a given when doing business today.

Even if you're not planning to sell directly online, a Web site can help you gain new customers, serve existing customers better, and streamline costs and operations. In fact, most business-to-business Web sites are established for a dual purpose—to sell products and services, either directly or indirectly, and to provide information. Here are some other important reasons for having a Web site:

1. The Internet is the first place your target market turns when researching products and services information. No Web site? Not to worry; a competitor will be more than happy to take the business from you.

2. A Web site empowers you to run your business 24 hours a day, 7 days a week. While you're home in bed, your Web site could be bringing in new leads or making sales through the wee hours in the morning. When many people make a purchase, they do so for that instant gratification. Give it to them.

3. A Web site can expand your customer base to get new customers! Your Web site is available to anyone, anywhere. Not only can you use your Web site to reach out to geographic markets outside your regular service area, but you can reach out to new markets in other countries cost-effectively. Even within your regular service area, there are all kinds of opportunity. You will have people who find you through the traditional Yellow Pages, but by having a Web site, you now open the door for would-be customers to find you online.

4. A Web site can build your business's reputation. Your Web site can help establish your business as credible and trustworthy; it helps build consumer confidence when you portray a professional image.

5. A Web site helps create a more level playing field. Every business can have a Web site, and that Web site can be as professional as the big players' sites.

6. A Web site is an effective, affordable way to advertise your business. Advertising runs on TV, on the radio, or in print are gone in a blip and can cost a lot more to execute for a lot less in the results department. Your Web site never stops advertising for you.

7. A Web site can help lower your costs. It's cheaper to update a Web site than to reprint a brochure to reflect the latest product changes. You can do business without hiring extra employees; you don't need to pay for postage. You get the idea.

8. A Web site can improve communications with all of your audiences. Your Web site can provide the most current information about your business to your customers, vendors, and employees.

9. A Web site provides valuable information to your customers. Your Web site is the perfect location to provide your target market with access to your brochure, case studies, white papers, interactive demos, and more. The information on your Web site can be updated on the fly so that it is always up-to-date.

10. A Web site can sell stuff. Your Web site can be another point of sale for your business!

11. A Web site can be used to learn about your target market. Your Web site is a natural place to gather demographic, geographic, and behavioral data about your target market that you can then use to generate more business. People sign up for newsletters, create user accounts that contain their personal information and buying patterns, participate in surveys, and so on. Extremely powerful Web Analytics packages exist today that enable you to monitor everything related to your Web site so that you can learn what works, what doesn't, and what to do better; everything is measurable.

12. A Web site can be used for employee recruitment. Including career information on your Web site can attract highly qualified employees you otherwise might not have found.

13. Your competitors have a Web site. Why would you let your competitors get a leg up on you?

14. Your competitors do not have a Web site. Why wouldn't you want to get a leg up on the competition?

15. Your Web site can provide great PR for your business by speaking directly to the media.

16. Your Web site can be a great source of networking for you and your business. A Web site has the potential to open the door to new vendors and partnership opportunities you never thought possible.

17. Your Web site can help you provide better customer service. Frequently Asked Questions, Support Forums, Online Chat, Contact Information, Software Patches and Updates, Tutoring Videos, Downloadable Manuals—the list goes on. Your Web site is a natural place to provide your customers with self-service access to customer service–related material and can alleviate some of the burden for your employees.

18. Your Web site can be used for branding and generating awareness for your business, product line, and so on.

19. Your Web site can be used to showcase stuff! A Web site is far more engaging than a brochure will ever be, and you can do so much more with a Web site to help sell your products or services. Showcase your success stories and case studies in order to share them with the world.

20. Your Web site can make a great sales tool. Your sales team can use your Web site to help sell your products and services. Your Web site can be home to many interactive items that your sales team can use when on site with a potential client, share over the phone, or send as a link in an email message such as a link to examples of how you helped a related client in the past. Your Web site can also include the most recent sales material that your team can use at any time to help ensure that everyone always has access to the most current material.

We could go on and on about all of the convincing reasons to have a Web site—it's even good for the environment. A Web site should be the hub for your marketing efforts, which leads us into the next topic. Now that you understand the value of having a Web site, what kind of Web site do you need?

Know the Purpose of Your Web Site

Web sites tend to do a number of things at the same time, such as provide information, sell products, and offer customer service content; however, there should be a fundamental purpose as the driver behind the Web site. A site with an unclear message will not perform nearly as well as a Web site that is sure in its intentions. That's why you take the time to define your target market, establish objectives for your Web site, and relate it all back to your business and its products or services. Know the purpose of your Web site and develop it based on that.

Lead Generation

Lead generation is a common business reason to have a Web site, particularly when your products or services are not impulse purchases or are of a more complex nature such that each customer's needs are unique and you must speak with the potential customer.

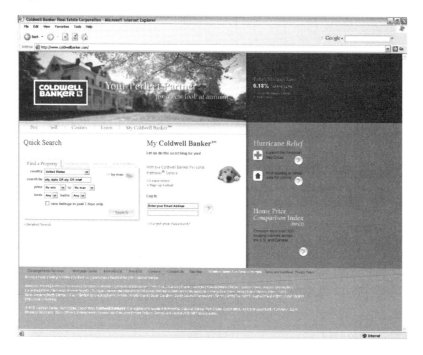

Figure 4.1. Coldwell Banker's home page.

Car dealerships, insurance services, and franchise opportunities are three examples of operations that use lead-generation Web sites to benefit their businesses.

The real estate industry is another example where lead-generation sites are highly effective. Coldwell Banker, pictured in Figure 4.1, is an example of a real estate services company. The primary objective of this Web site is to qualify leads from people looking to buy or sell a home. Potential customers have the opportunity to make contact with an agent from many points throughout the Web site.

The idea behind a lead-generation Web site is to capture qualified sales leads by getting the target market to make contact with you. With a lead-generation Web site, you shorten the sales cycle by giving your customer the power to educate themselves. Before you ever speak to a potential customer, you already have several questions answered through requests on your Web site.

The more efficient and better marketed your lead-generation Web site is, the easier it becomes to close the sale and the less it costs to generate leads. Wouldn't it be nice to have to do less cold calling and prepare less print material?

Online Sales

Online sales and transactions are another great business reason behind a Web site. E-commerce generates billions and billions of dollars each year. Your store might be open 9 a.m. to 9 p.m., but your customer might have a hankering to make a purchase at 2 in the morning. Keep your business open and sell your wares 24/7. An e-commerce Web site can be applied to many industries, with the most recognized being travel and retail. Everyone knows the names Amazon.com, Dell, and Expedia. These are all wildly successful businesses largely driven by their strong Web presence.

Many, many small businesses see great success when they take their businesses online. AMOS Pewter (Figure 4.2) is one such example of an online retailer that is seeing the benefits in the bottom line.

Think about what type of site is needed for your business. Remember that people often research online and then make their purchase offline. In fact, the Internet influences far more offline sales than those produced from direct online purchases. Understand the needs of your market and tailor your site to your customer. Only then will you achieve the best results.

Figure 4.2. AMOS Pewter's Web site.

Don't Start Without a Plan

Before you embark on designing a new Web site, you should have an e-business and Internet marketing strategy. Know what you're getting into before you dive in head first—have a plan.

For the sake of argument, some common e-business strategy goals might be:

- Generate more business from direct online sales or sales influenced by the Internet.

- Increase your share of the target market's wallet.

- Increase overall conversion ratios.

- Increase repeat business and build relationships with the target market through improved customer satisfaction, loyalty, and retention initiatives.

- Increase awareness and educate the target market about the company.

- Increase targeted Web site traffic.

- Reduce internal costs by reducing inefficiencies and expenditures to increase overall profit margins.

Earlier in the book we said that your online strategy should take into account your business objectives, your budget, your target market, and your products/services, as these components will serve as the foundation of your strategy which will in turn be one of the building blocks for how you approach your Web presence.

The Q2C Model—The Genetics of a Great Web Site

When potential customers come to your Web site, you have but mere seconds to communicate your message to them and let them know they're in the right place. Once you have potential customers' attention, you need to keep it and get them to take the next step and follow through on the action you want them to partake in on your site. How do you do that?

Here's the thing. It doesn't matter if you're in healthcare, travel, retail, or professional services. It doesn't matter if you're creating a lead-generation Web site, an e-commerce Web site, a customer service Web site, or an information-based Web site. It doesn't matter if you're creating a large-scale Web

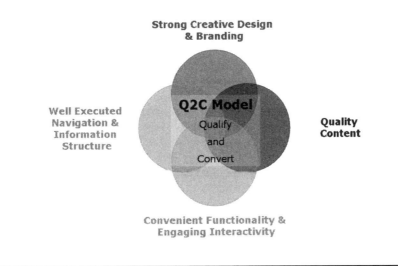

Figure 4.3. The Q2C Model.

site, a mini site for a specific product line, or a landing page to capitalize on a single sales opportunity. The genetic make-up of a successful Web site will always follow the Q2C Model—from qualifying the prospect to capturing the conversion (Figure 4.3).

The genetic make-up of a great site must address four areas:

1. Design

2. Navigation

3. Content

4. Functionality.

How you execute the model will be unique to your business needs and the needs of your customers, but every aspect of the Q2C Model must be addressed in order to create that great Web presence that works for you.

Strong Creative Design and Branding

According to a recent research report by Consumer WebWatch (*How Do People Evaluate a Web Site's Credibility? Results from a Large Study*, 2002), 46.1 percent of a Web site's credibility is based first on its look and feel or graphic design. People will "judge a book by its cover," so to speak, when they first come upon your Web site. People like stuff that looks good.

Strong creative design and branding is the ability of the Web site to communicate the value proposition and positioning of the brand through visuals. The design of a Web site must be engaging, promote a memorable experience, extend the reach of the brand through the Web site, and be consistent with the message delivered through traditional means.

Design your site for your target market—what will make them respond favorably? These are just a few considerations that go into a great design that you should keep in mind.

Think about the quality of the design work. In addition to visual appeal, you need to consider the functional and performance aspects of the design. You want your design to naturally guide the eyes of your potential customers, and you want it to be easy for them to take the desired action on your Web site.

For example, the presentation of content should be easy for people to scan, meaning that fonts should be easy to read and you should choose colors that will not cause any problems for your target market. Using dark text on a light-colored background is much easier to read, or scan, than a Web site that uses a patterned background design.

The heavier your design, the longer it will take to load in the end user's browser. In some cases heavy, image-intensive designs work wonders, but in most cases this is going to cause problems. Internet users have a relatively low attention span, so you have only a few seconds to capture their attention. If your homepage is still trying to load after 60 seconds, forget it; your potential customer gave up 54 seconds ago. A good designer thinks about how the site will perform once it has been coded and takes this into consideration when creating a site design.

The design for a Web site must help portray the experience. If a beach is an important draw for an area, then the accompanying Web site will want to do more than just show a sub-par picture of an empty beach. The site should have a high-quality shot of that beach on a hot summer day that includes members of their target market enjoying themselves in order to give people an experience they can relate to and build the desire to participate.

Did you know that around 10 percent of the general population are red–green color blind? If you are designing a Web site playing off of these two colors, many people might not be able to differentiate between the colors.

Did you know many people automatically ignore anything online that looks like a banner ad? Yup, it's so popular the phrase "banner blindness" has been coined to describe how people tend not to notice things that look like a banner or are placed in locations on a page where a banner ad would usually be placed. People ignore blinking and flash text, too.

If you really want to irritate your target market but good, make sure your site forces horizontal scrolling to see everything on the page. This brings us to an important point. Think about screen resolution when designing your Web site. If your Web site is designed for 1024 x 768 and higher, you could be eliminating upwards of 25 percent of your market, generally speaking, who prefer a screen resolution of 800 x 600. Again, a good designer will help you make the right design-related decisions for your site.

If you are looking to appeal to international markets, then you should design around those individual audiences to reflect cultural differences and preferences. In China, the color red is representative of happiness. In Egypt, the color red is associated with death.

All we want you to take away from this section is that you should know for whom you are designing. The quality of the design of your Web site plays an extremely influential role in building credibility and trust with your potential customer. Design for your customer. Take the time to get it right. Be inviting.

Well-Executed Navigation and Information Structure

When I click a link, do I end up where I expect to be? Organization is a beautiful thing. Well-executed navigation and information structure is essential to successful conversions through your Web site.

According to the same research report by Consumer WebWatch cited earlier (*How Do People Evaluate a Web Site's Credibility? Results from a Large Study,* 2002), 28.5 percent of people assigned significant weight to information structure when assigning credibility to a Web site. What does this mean? Sites that are easy to navigate are viewed as more credible.

A site must be credible in order to drive favorable actions from your target market. The navigation and information structure for a Web site must be logical, focused around the key objectives of the target market, easy to use, free of errors, and consistent throughout the Web site.

A couple questions to consider when thinking about site navigation are:

- *Is the Web site easy to use?* The navigation should remain consistent throughout the Web site for familiarity and should naturally guide users to complete their desired goals. Navigation links should be clearly labeled so that there is no frustrating guesswork.

- *Does the Web site offer navigation alternatives?* A good Web site should give the target market more than one way to navigate, such as text link alternatives for users with accessibility issues, an HTML alternative to Flash, a Site Map, perhaps a site search to help find items in a product catalogue and bread crumb navigation so the user can follow their trail. Remember, good navigation also helps search engines index your Web site!

Figure 4.4.   Mahone Bay's Web site.

In Figure 4.4, notice how the navigation choices on the Mahone Bay home page immediately qualify the target market to lead them into the appropriate sections of the Web site. No effort is needed on the part of the user to "figure out" what is behind the various navigation options. Everything is clear.

Where, what, and how you place items on a page is an important factor in defining site navigation too. Making links in body copy obvious will ensure that they get clicked. If something is extremely important, then place it prominently above the page fold (where you start to scroll vertically to see the rest of the page) to capture the most attention. Too many options on a page will confuse people, so you want to keep your options simple and related to the task at hand; you will get more sales this way.

When developing a Web site, it is important that you develop a navigation structure that will work for your business. Put in the time to properly plan your site architecture. There are industry professionals and usability experts who can assist you in preparing the right architecture for your Web site.

Quality Content

You're not going to get by on good looks and form alone. You need to have substance to the copy on your Web site.

You can have a great-looking Web site that does not produce any results because the content of the site is not sufficient or focused to convert the customer. Copy on a Web site must address the needs of the target market; must be complete, useful, accurate, and persuasive; should speak to the brand and needs to be presented with clarity and be easily scanned; people scan, not read, looking for something that piques their interest.

Good copy builds credibility, trust, and ultimately sales for an organization. Copy is what transmits the personality of an organization to the target market where they will decide whether or not to do business with a company. In addition, quality page copy is essential to ranking well with search engines.

Writing for the Web is different from writing for print. Consumers behave differently online. In particular, people read much more slowly online. When preparing page copy, there are many things to consider, which is why it is recommended that a copywriter with reputable Web experience be hired.

Is your Web site written for your target market and are you answering all of their questions? This is the question you should be asking yourself of your content. For example, leave .PDFs to big documents that are intended to be printed—say everything you need to say on your site instead of creating an obstacle for your potential customer. If you're selling something, you should post your prices online; people are going to want to know the cost of your items, and why would you make them "work" for it? When talking about products, be sure to discuss relevant benefits of the products' features so that potential buyers can envision actually using the product. We could go on and on, but there already are entire books on the subject out there. We will leave you with this tip though; don't be boring, but ease off the marketese nonsense!

Convenient Functionality and Engaging Interactivity

It's not just what you do, but how you do it. If you're going to get something out of your Web site, you have to provide the functionality for the potential customer to take an action, and you have to make sure everything works as it should. Everything must be easy for the user.

Let's consider a hotel or hotel chain as an example. The right look and feel, excellent navigation, and useful information present a convincing picture for the Web site. We know, though, that an information-only Web site will not get the job done. The target market expects to be able to make a reservation, download a brochure, plan their trip online, and so on, quickly and easily with no barriers preventing them from doing so. If the Web site is too slow, they'll give up. If the Web site generates an error, they'll lose confidence.

A hotel Web site must extend different touch points to the target market, allowing them access to self-service tools (e.g., interactive package builders, maps and directions, etc.) and engaging features to capture leads, drive immediate sales, and promote consumer loyalty (e.g., through permission marketing, access to a rewards program online for an individual business, etc.).

Here are some examples of key and value-added functionality options for a hotel:

- Viral Marketing (e.g. "Tell a friend" functionality for a particular page, special offers, newsletter)

- Online Reservations for Accommodations and Area Attractions (e.g., from a low-cost basic form with information collection fields so you can manually process reservations to a fully capable real-time reservations engine fully integrated with the property management system, loyalty program, and so on)

- My Account/Guest Profile (e.g., personalized user accounts to allow customers to change personal information, change/cancel reservations, manage their preferences, view purchase history, or save their trip itinerary to give customers complete control over their online travel experience)

- Vacation Planner/Trip Builder (e.g., customizable vacation packages with the hotel accommodations at the center of the experience.)

- Self-Serve Customer Service Applications (e.g., ability to download brochures, partake in real-time chat, access searchable FAQs, easily print page content, view real-time weather conditions, use a real-time currency converter)

- Engaging Tours (e.g., sell the appeal of the hotel or hotels through a photo slideshow that tells a story, 360-degree tours, interactive webmercials)

- Permission Marketing (e.g., keep in contact with existing and potential customers through email and send them special offers, events at the hotel, and so forth).

Odds are that not everything is going to be a priority, and you may not have the resources to tackle it all, anyway. You must make an informed decision about what functionality is necessary to sell your business to your potential customers that you can afford. A Web site grows over time, so you can gradually expand (or reduce if the case may be) your approach over time.

The functionality of your Web site must be unique to your business and the needs of your target market. On a retail Web site, customers will be able to view complete details about your products, understand pricing and shipping, and get a good view of the product from multiple angles since they cannot hold it in their hands and be able to make the purchase. After the purchase, the customer should automatically receive a confirmation, or receipt, by e-mail so that he or she knows the order is in good hands. You will want to keep in touch with your customers to encourage them to come back and purchase again, so you will want to give the target market opportunities to sign-on to receive e-mail communications from you–right from the checkout.

On the other side of the coin, don't include everything you can possibly include on your site just because you can. What you do not want to do is overwhelm the user in the middle of the purchase process with 20 other, unrelated products that will distract them and potentially put a halt to their current order.

Equally important to functionality is the performance of the Web site itself. This drills down into how the site and all of its supporting functions are coded. Users will quickly become frustrated by a Web site that generates errors on a regular basis or that does not load within a reasonable time period. Likewise, focusing on only one dynamic of the market can frustrate other market segments.

Broadband access is rapidly becoming adopted in North America, but many Internet users go online via dial-up connections, so building a Web site entirely in Macromedia Flash with heavy animations can exclude a large portion of the market, and not just because of demanding performance requirements. Sites built entirely in Flash tend to force the target market to sit through the same sequences over and over again, which tries the patience of many a customer who merely want to get to the desired information as quickly as possible.

One of the biggest concerns with building a Web site is whom to build your Web site for when you want to appeal to the masses. W3Schools maintains reliable data on browser usage, screen resolutions, and operating systems on a month-by-month basis that allows you to observe trends. You can learn more about browser trends on the W3Schools Web site at *http:// www.w3schools.com/browsers/browsers_stats.asp.*

When developing a Web site, it should be standard practice to factor in clean code that is fast and error free, taking into account cross-browser compatibility, a speedy load time, and the like. Remember:

- The lion's share of the Internet population is still on a dial-up connection and you need to make sure your Web site loads within several seconds for this audience. Many people live in areas where a broadband connection is not an option.

- At a minimum, your Web site should be designed to work properly at a screen resolution of 800 x 600. Many people operate at this screen resolution, and it is generally considered best practice to design with this resolution as a starting point to make sure your Web site best accommodates everybody.

- Not everyone uses the latest Windows and the newest version of Internet Explorer. You need to check your development efforts across the platforms used by your customers. A Tool like BrowserCam (*http://www.browsercam.com/*) can show you how your Web site appears across a plethora of browsers and operating systems to help you make the necessary adjustments so that your Web site displays equally well for all.

Respect your users and make sure your Web site and all it has to offer works for them, not against them.

When all is said and done, you want a Web site that is going to bring you success. Success for you might be defined as:

- Increased sales

- Increased lead generation

- Increased repeat business and customer loyalty

- Increased customer satisfaction

- Increased brand awareness.

Success will be achieved only if:

1. Your Web site is relevant to the needs of the customer,

2. The customer trusts your business, including privacy and security matters, and

3. The customer is convinced of the value of the products/services offered through your site.

Addressing each area in the Q2C Model for a great Web site will put you on the path to having a credible Web site.

At this point, it should be clear that putting together a successful Web presence is an involved process that requires proper planning and skills. In the next section we look at the steps to follow to create your Web site.

Eight Strategic Steps to Developing a Successful Web Site

Approaching the Q2C Model can be summarized into an eight-step executable plan. At all stages of the process you should be checking and testing everything so that the end product is everything it should be.

1. Do Your Research

Understand your objectives, your target market, your products/services, and the competitive landscape.

Earlier in the book we discussed the importance of knowing your environment before diving in. You want to be as informed as possible. You can review market research studies, conduct a competitive analysis, host focus groups, hold interviews, run surveys, and more, to educate yourself before starting to piece together the architecture of your Web site. Look at other Web sites to see what they're doing and what works.

2. Prepare Your Strategy

Plan your strategy to create a convincing architecture for your Web site that speaks directly to your target market and drives the action you want them to take.

In short, put together a blueprint for your Web site. Names like "information architecture," "Web Site Storyboard," and "Wire frames" are common terminology for a site blueprint.

We use the term "Web Site Storyboard" when talking about a blueprint for a Web site. Putting together a Web Site Storyboard is an absolutely essential step in developing a Web site, so we will spend a bit of time on this topic.

Would you just wing building a home? Of course not. You need to see where everything is going to go and how it all comes together in order to understand what you're getting and what it's going to cost to build it, so that the contractors actually have a plan to follow to build it.

A Web Site Storyboard is a complete visual representation or blueprint of how all Web site components are tied together and are laid out to produce a solid, functional Web site that is designed in accordance with your budget and strategic objectives.

The storyboard for a Web site illustrates the navigational structure of your site, dynamically driven pages, repeat traffic–generation elements, viral marketing elements, and permission marketing elements, as well as the recommended content for each page of the site.

Everything is laid out on paper before any development costs are incurred to make sure the needs of all stakeholders are met. It's much cheaper to revise a Web site on paper than it is to go back to change the design and re-code everything.

3. Design Your Graphical User Interface and Prepare Persuasive Content

What's the Web site going to look like? What is the Web site going to say exactly?

You need to create the atmosphere that captures your audience and doesn't let go. Follow your Web Site Storyboard to create a conceptual design that appeals to your customers.

Before moving into development, you should have the content of your Web site prepared and organized according to the Web Site Storyboard. This makes the development process much easier as the project team spends less time and fewer resources trying to hunt down the missing blanks.

4. Build the Web Site and Supporting Applications

This is where your dream is realized and the site comes together. Here the development team will develop the site using HTML, Flash, XHTML, Java, .Net, XML, PHP—whatever the technology needs may be!

Coding of the Web site should be based on your audience requirements and best practices. Depending on who your audience is, how you build your Web site will vary. If you're talking to game players, your Web site will likely employ the latest technology in a media-intensive environment with lots of videos and interactive components. If you're talking to a more mature market, then accessibility might be your prime concern.

When coding, you must keep in line with cross-browser platform requirements, search engine optimization techniques, optimal site performance, and usability standards. Test everything.

5. Launch the Web Site

Make it live! Test and publish the Web site to the host server. Before releasing the Web site to the public, quadruple-check everything. You need to make sure transactions are handled properly, that e-mails are going where they should, and that everything simply works properly.

6. Market Your Web Site

What good is your new lead-generation site, promotional landing page, or e-commerce site if no one knows about it? You must market your Web site through both online and office mediums that reach your customer. This book and its counterpart, *101 Ways to Promote Your Web Site,* tell you how to do just that.

7. Measure Your Success

Monitor the success of your Web site and online advertising initiatives. What's working? What's not and why not? What could be improved? Further in this book we will talk about Web site traffic analysis and metrics to help you make informed business decisions.

8. Test, Refine, Test, Refine. . .

Quite simply, do more of what works and less of what doesn't. There is always room for improvement. Your Web site will constantly evolve and grow over time to adapt to changing consumer needs and changes within your business.

A stale Web site is a dead Web site. You need to keep your Web site fresh and continually make improvements to increase conversions and generate customer loyalty. Retain your customers.

Making the Right Choices

A Web site is a marketing medium, but it is much more than just an online brochure for your organization—it must be interactive and engaging. A Web site is a strategic tool that plays a critical role in the success of all different types of businesses and organizations in the new economy.

There are specialists available in all areas of Web site development—if someone claims to be able to do it all, they're lying. Nobody is the best at everything. The graphic designer is not going to be an ideal copywriter as well. The software or HTML developer is not going to make the ideal designer.

It is important to surround yourself with the right people. Your project team might consist of:

1. Project manager with Web site and database application development experience

2. Graphic designer(s) who specialize in Web design. No, this is not the same person who does your brochures.

3. Database developer(s) with experience in Web applications

4. Web site developer(s) who has plenty of experience and doesn't even need to think about coding for different browsers, potential users, and the search engines

5. Copywriter with experience in writing for an online audience. There is a big difference in writing for print and in writing for the Web.

6. Usability and marketing experts to guide the strategy for the Web site

7. Third-party application vendors such as a storefront solution provider or e-mail marketing suppliers. These vendors focus on nothing but being the best in their field.

8. Your internal team of stakeholders who understand your business better than any outside individual ever could.

9. Your customers–get those who will be using the site involved.

In this book we're not trying to teach you how to build a Web site. What we want to do is educate you that a lot goes into preparing a great Web site and that it is worth the investment to hire professionals with experience. Sure, it will cost you more up front than the Joe Blow out of his basement, but in the end the results are going to be there. Working with the right team will make you more money and will save you money down the road, and you'll certainly experience fewer headaches.

5

Campaign Execution

Proper campaign execution can mean the difference between online success and failure. Too often, businesses rush into launching their online campaigns without taking the time to think their strategy through. To reiterate the points stressed earlier in this book, if you don't take the foundation of your online activities into consideration—that is, your objectives, target markets, and products/services—your campaigns will not generate the results that you are looking for. The foundation supports everything from selecting the most appropriate communication channels to the messaging and tonality used in your campaigns. You could have the most ideal Web site for your target market, which would be a beautiful thing, but if you can't get the "right" traffic to that Web site, it serves little purpose.

In this section of *3G Marketing on the Internet,* we will review items to consider when developing your campaigns, including:

- Working with the right channels

- Making sure you score before you shoot—campaign preparation

- Consistency is key!

- Developing a winning landing page

- Making PPC (pay-per-click) campaigns work for you

- Getting noticed in the world of spam

- Working with the right tools

- Designing effective e-mail promotions.

Working With the Right Channels

There is not really a set formula for selecting which communication channels are appropriate for your business, but there is a process that should be followed when determining which channels you should be working with, and by this part of the book I'll bet you know what it is. Remember that in Chapter 4 of this book it was stressed how the foundation plays a role in everything that you do online? Well, selecting how you are going to speak to your prospective clients is no different.

With all of the different ways there are to communicate with your target market, it is amazing how many businesses are *solely* focused on using search engines to drive traffic to their site—and for good reason. Search engines are typically responsible for driving 60–80 percent of Web site traffic. With that being said, there are so many other channels available online that are often overlooked—particularly by small to medium-sized businesses. These channels, which were outlined in Chapter 3 of this book, can drive an equal amount of targeted traffic to your Web site. But how do you select the right channels for your business?

The first thing to understand is that several online marketing channels require a monetary investment, whereas there are others that offer businesses a more cost-effective way to promote their sites. The latter often require an investment of time rather than money; however, the results can be outstanding. For example, devoting time to the development of your company's link strategy can take a significant amount of time; however, the investment of time not only will increase your reach on the Internet to your prospective clients, but it will also increase your link popularity. The increase in link popularity will boost your rankings in the major search engines—particularly Google. Link-strategy development is a technique that should be implemented by all organizations regardless of their budget; however, it often is overlooked.

Developing a link strategy is just one example of a cost-effective way to promote your Web site. Regardless of your budget, there are options available to you. Yes, search engine marketing should be a component of your online marketing strategy; that goes without saying. Optimizing your Web site for high search engine placement isn't something that just anyone can do, either. It takes time to learn the different techniques involved in properly optimizing a Web site. If you are committed to achieving search engine marketing success and have little or no knowledge in this area, you should allocate a portion of your budget to having a professional take care of this for you. The key is to determine how you want to reach your target market online and then determine what is feasible, what can be handled in house, and what should be outsourced.

When selecting your online communication channels, you have to ask yourself three basic questions. These questions include:

- Will the referral traffic from this communication channel help me to support my online marketing objectives?

- Does the referral traffic from this communication channel match the profile of one of my defined target market segments?

- Is the referral traffic from this communication channel interested in the products or services that I am promoting on my Web site?

Now if you answer "no" to any of the above, you are wasting your time, and potentially your money too. Similar to how this foundation helped you to build your Web site, these same principles apply to the proactive marketing of your site. The three principles work together. If you are analyzing a communication channel that does not speak to your target market, the chance that referring traffic will be interested in your products or services is small—even nonexistent. This will result in the lack of support of your set marketing objectives; thus you're wasting your time altogether. Still seem a little too simple? That's because it is. It's not a complicated process to understand.

In order to follow this process, you need to ensure that you thoroughly understand both your own environment (see the following section in this chapter) as well as the environment of those channels you are evaluating. If you're evaluating a communication channel, look for an advertising center on the Web site or at least some sort of a demographic profile for the site's target visitors. Figure 5.1 outlines MSN's Advertising Center, a very thorough component of their Web site that highlights their audience profile, their reach, and why you should advertise with them, along with other research to assist users with understanding the effectiveness of advertising on their network. Of course, this information is prepared to convince you to want to advertise with MSN; however, the general statistics provided within this component of their Web site will provide you with a general idea of whether this channel is appropriate for you or not.

Not every online communication channel will have a detailed profile of its Web site visitors. In fact, most won't even know where to begin when profiling their visitors, with the exception of those that offer sites targeted

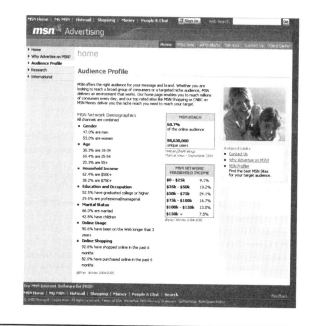

Figure 5.1. MSN's AdCenter provides users with detailed advertising specs.

toward a specific audience (e.g., travel reviews, home decorating, etc.). I'm sure you all have been approached hundreds of times by e-mail marketers or telemarketers trying to convince you to purchase online advertising on their sites. Usually it goes something like: "We are the premiere source for <insert topic> information and receive *millions of hits* every day." What does this really mean? Everybody is the "ultimate" source for a particular type of information. You can usually weed out the less valuable communication channels simply by asking the right questions. If they have no answers for you, chances are they don't really know what they're doing. Sample questions to ask include the following:

- Can you provide me with a profile of the different segments of users who visit your Web site?

- How many *unique visits* does your site receive on a monthly basis?

- How many subscribers does your newsletter target? How qualified is your database of subscribers and by what means did you generate your subscriber list?

- What are you currently doing to promote your Web site on the Internet?

- Could you provide me with references of other, similar businesses that currently are advertising with your organization?

- What kind of reporting do you offer? Do you provide monthly reports outlining the number of referrals your Web site generates?

These are just a few sample questions that you should always ask any advertiser that is trying to solicit online advertising from you. It will be apparent whether or not they know what they are doing by their response. If they stutter on their response, they could (a) not know what they are doing or (b) simply not be qualified to provide an accurate response. If you feel strongly about the opportunity, give them the benefit of the doubt and let them send you further information. Hey, maybe you were the first person to ever ask for such information. If so, you're doing them a favor, as you're helping them to improve their own process.

Making Sure You Score Before You Shoot— Campaign Preparation

Campaign preparation is as critical as selecting the right channels for communicating with your target market. You could have selected the ideal communication channels for your business, but if you execute a sloppy campaign you not only will not achieve your desired results, but you also risk tarnishing your target market's perception of your brand. So what are the fundamental steps that should be taken when preparing for your next campaign? Keep in mind that depending on the channels you choose, the exact requirements will differ; the steps outlined below provide a high-level overview of the process that any business should follow.

To illustrate this process, we are going to follow the same steps taken by White Point Vacation Club (*www.whitepointvacationclub.com*), a sought-after timeshare operation targeting prospects who are 26 years of age or older with a household income of $60,000 or more. White Point is targeting users through various online communication channels, but for the purpose of this explanation, we are going to focus discussions around the implementation of targeted PPC campaigns.

Action Item #1: Campaign Foundation

Yes, we are going to ask it again. What are the objectives of the campaign? Which segments of your market are you targeting with the campaign? What are you promoting and how should this product or service be presented to your target market in order to get them to respond to your campaign?

In the case of White Point, the primary objective of the campaign is to encourage prospective timeshare owners to visit the resort for a stress-free weekend to experience all that White Point has to offer. Users are presented with an enticing offer, and upon acceptance of the offer they agree to take a preview tour of the White Point Vacation Club vacation ownership opportunity. This is the primary objective of each campaign—tour generation.

How does the product being promoted—vacation ownership—have to be positioned to the target market? Well, given the nature of the communication channel—PPC advertising—users will be targeted based on their behavior as dictated by their search criteria. We'll talk a little bit more about this later in this chapter.

Action Item #2: Matching the Message With the Desire

What is the message that you are going to communicate to your target market to convince them to click through to learn more about your products and services? If you want to communicate with your market, you need to position your message around their views and desires as they relate to your product. If your message coincides with the users' desires, then the probability that they will click through to learn more about your offering is very good. Similarly, those visitors who happen to stumble across your message who do not share this specific desire will not click on your ad—these are the lost causes.

Moving along with the example, since White Point is targeting users through PPC advertising campaigns, it is important to segment users based on their search behavior prior to developing their message for their PPC campaigns. What would a prospective client for the vacation ownership product be searching for online? There are multiple scenarios, keyword themes, etc., that are all valid answers to this question. To keep things simple, let's simply assume we are targeting those users who are looking to take a summer vacation to Atlantic Canada—a popular destination for travelers from around the world. Using this particular segment, one must do the necessary research to determine the combinations of keywords related to the theme of "Atlantic Canada Vacation" that users are querying in the major search engines. Once the keywords are selected, it's simply a matter of preparing your PPC ads to speak to the desires of your target market (See Figure 5.2)—something we are going to cover in more detail later in this chapter.

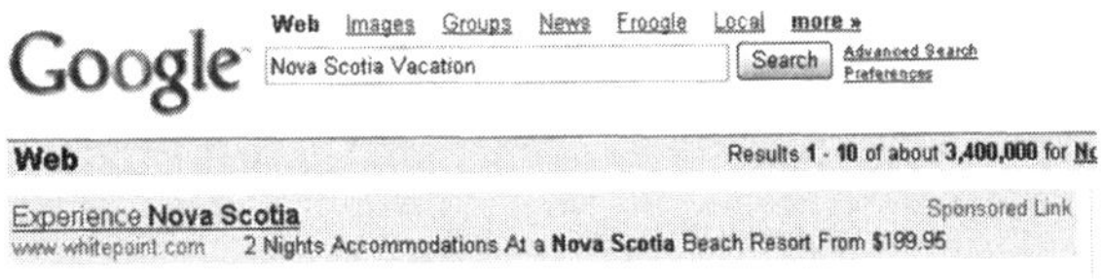

Figure 5.2. White Point Vacation Club (*www.whitepointvacationclub.com*) communicates with its target market using targeted PPC campaigns.

Action Item #3: Make Sure All the Tools Are in Place

It's truly sad how many businesses invest time and money into implementing campaigns, get their message in front of their target market, and yet do not follow through on the promise of the offer. For example, how many online advertisements have you ever clicked on that promise a spectacular offer of some sort only to direct you to the homepage of the business's Web site, where you are left thinking "what about that great deal?" It happens too often.

What about those inquiry forms that you complete online to see if you "qualify" for a specific offer or promotion? Users visit the form, complete the form, and are left thinking "what happens now?" The bottom line is, if you want to keep the attention of your prospects and increase your conversions, you have to be sure that the proper tools, Web site elements, etc., are in place to ensure that your prospective clients complete the task that you are asking them to do—whether it be to fill out an online registration form or buy a product online.

So what are the tips, tools, and techniques that should be taken into consideration when implementing an online campaign? Consider the following:

Privacy and Security: Businesses that succeed in their online marketing endeavors tend to leverage the success of their campaigns by prominently displaying their privacy and security policies. Since most campaigns result in a user's submitting personal data of some sort, people like to know how their personal information will be handled. In the world of spam, Internet users are very reluctant to hand over their details to a company or organization that does not explain how their information will be used. Privacy and security policies help in building trust and confidence among your target market. These days, people are inundated with junk e-mail and are reluctant at the best of times to provide their e-mail address. Regardless of what you are promoting, if you are asking your prospects for information, make sure to explain your privacy policy and security policy, and display any certificates of authentication (e.g., BBBOnline, VeriSign, etc.).

Landing Pages: Landing pages are the foundation for any online marketing initiative; their purpose is to minimize distractions and focus the target market on accomplishing the goal presented in your original campaign advertisement. When you promote an offer online, whether it be a banner ad, newsletter promotion, or pay-to-play campaign, you want to maximize the results of your effort. When done properly, a targeted landing page for an ad can greatly increase conversions, which is the portion of your target market who act on your offer. The same applies to offline promotions. If you are driving traffic to your Web site through offline means, it is important to send the user to a landing page. Send them to the offer. Tips for designing winning landing pages can be found later in this chapter.

Autoresponders: One of the major benefits of using an autoresponder is the immediate response—24 hours a day, 7 days a week, and 365 days a year—providing immediate gratification for the recipient. Autoresponders are also a real time-saver, eliminating the need for manual responses for many routine requests. One big advantage with today's autoresponders is the ability to schedule multiple messages at predetermined intervals. The first response can go immediately, with a second message timed to go two days after the first, a third message to go five days after the second, and so on. Market research tells you that a prospect needs to be exposed to your message multiple times to become a motivated buyer or registrant. Keeping your brand and your offer in front of your target market will increase the likelihood that they will convert.

Conversion Tracking Tools: True, there are numerous ways in which you can track your campaign conversion ratios—some being more primitive than others, yet all delivering the same end results. For example, if you are running a banner ad campaign on a high traffic content site, one could simply track the amount of referrals generated from the campaign and the amount of inquiries that are generated as a result of the landing page and a unique 1-800 number associated with the promotion. Do the math and you can easily find your traffic conversion ratio by dividing the amount of inquiries generated by the amount of exposure generated for the offer.

Again, depending on the type of campaign you are implementing, your budget for implementation tools, and the nature of how you are tracking your visitors (e.g., lead generation, sales, etc.), the tools and techniques you implement will vary. The different PPC advertising models that are available (e.g., Google AdWords, Yahoo Search Marketing Solutions, etc.) offer free conversion-tracking scripts that enable advertisers to monitor visitor conversions simply by placing a small script on the page you want your visitors to

						Avg.		Avg.	Conv.	
☐ Keyword	Status [?]	Max CPC Bid	Clicks	Impr.	CTR	CPC	Cost	Pos	Rate ▼	Cost/Conv.
Search Total			46	2,122	2.1%	$0.78	$35.80	1.6	4.35%	$17.80
Content Total [?]			70	72,115	0.09%	$0.97	$67.84	2.3	1.43%	$67.84
☐ [Nova Scotia Resorts]	Active	$1.50	3	18	16.6%	$0.69	$2.07	1.1	33.33%	$2.07
☐ [nova scotia hotels]	Active	$1.50	30	942	3.1%	$0.72	$21.43	1.1	3.33%	$21.43

Figure 5.3. Monitor your conversion ratios using the AdWords control panel.

reach after completing an assigned task (e.g., thank you page, order confirmation page, etc.). Figure 5.3 illustrates the AdWords control panel that enables advertisers to monitor their conversion rates for a given campaign.

The point is that you must have the tools in place to track the actual performance of your campaigns. If you're not monitoring conversions, what is the point of advertising? We've seen so many companies get so excited over the exposure that they receive online in terms of the number of visitors coming to the site, the number of clicks their ads receive, and so on, but what is the point of all of this if you don't convert browsers to buyers? I mean, that's why you're marketing online, isn't it? You want to grow your business using the Internet. Tracking what's working, what's converting, and what isn't is the best way to identify what is working for your business and how you can monitor, modify, and improve your overall strategy to maximize its effectiveness.

White Point is trying to generate exposure for its mini-vacation offer using targeted PPC campaigns. When targeted users come across one of White Point's ads online, they are directed to a targeted landing page that is designed to coincide with the desire of the user. For example, if a user has conducted a query using the term "Nova Scotia Accommodations" he or she will be presented with a landing page that speaks to this desire and will distinguish the White Point experience from those of any other accommodations provider within the province of Nova Scotia. The story that the landing page presents (see Figure 5.4) is framed specifically to the needs of the target audience for the campaign. The story explains why White Point is the best option for the user and what distinguishes the resort property from other accommodation providers. This is accomplished by presenting a number of emotional appeals that ultimately will encourage the user to complete an online inquiry form to see if they qualify for the promotion. I use the term *qualify* because the landing page not only asks for the sale, but it also places a high level of urgency on the promotion. Using a "limited-time offer" statement on the promotion creates urgency, which will encourage the user to act

Figure 5.4. A sample landing page used to promote White Point Vacation Club.

now. How do we make the user comfortable with providing us with their personal information online? Simple. Proper positioning of a privacy policy and security statement on the landing page helps to alleviate any worries that a user may have about supplying the information.

Action Item #4: Monitor, Evaluate, and Modify

Most people think you monitor the effectiveness of a campaign only once the promotion is over, but this is not so. True, in the offline world when you launch a print campaign you monitor how effective the campaign is after it's over, but the difference is the fact that you can't change what has been put into circulation once it's printed. When launching a campaign online, this is not the case. For example, if you were to launch an extensive online advertising campaign using rich media banner advertisements, you could easily change the creative for the campaign halfway through the campaign if it proves that it is not generating the response that you are looking for—in most cases, anyway.

Whenever you launch a campaign, it's critical that you continuously monitor how your target market is responding to the campaign—not only determining if they are viewing your promotion, but are they responding to it? Are they completing the task that you have asked them to complete? If you simply implement a campaign and review its effectiveness once the campaign offer has expired, then you may find less than desirable results as the outcome. Alternatively, if you were to monitor the campaign's effectiveness during the ongoing implementation process, then you can identify its shortcomings before it's too late.

White Point spends a significant amount of time tracking both Web site activity and campaign activity. With numerous online and offline campaigns running concurrently to drive users to their Web site, it is critical to understand where Web site traffic is coming from and which programs are converting traffic to customers. Time is spent analyzing user behavior on the Web site, which calls to action are working, as well as common activity patterns among those users who actually convert to customers. Through gaining a clearer understanding of what motivates their visitors to react to a specific campaign, White Point can optimize its campaigns to increase the overall conversion ratios and maximize the online advertising budget.

Consistency Is Key!

No matter what online communication channels you are using to promote your business, it's critical that the message you're communicating to your target market is consistent across all mediums. How you position your brand, how you appeal to your target audience, and your overall communication strategy should be consistent throughout your marketing mix. You have to consider the different touch points that are available where your brand could reach your target market. For example, assume that you run an advertisement in a popular industry trade journal that is viewed by your target market regularly. Now, this ad may or may not drive users to your Web site, but what happens if these same members of your target market are reading an article on a popular industry-specific content site and view a banner ad for your business? If your communication strategy is consistent, the users eventually will link your online/offline ads together, which ultimately will bring the user to your site—something we know counts only if your site is prepared for the traffic.

It's important to stress that being consistent doesn't mean that you simply create your offline advertising in an online environment. As we all know by now, the Internet is very different from communicating to your offline audience. With technological limitations and researched user characteristics, it's important that you adapt your communication strategy to the medium.

Sure, it would be great to amuse your visitors with a large visual depicting humorous billboard advertisements that your offline market views repeatedly, but how does this same advertisement translate to an electronic medium? If a user is on your Web site, he or she most likely is there because of an interest in your product or service. So, while you communicate with users using a consistent communication strategy, it's critical that you acknowledge that it is at this point that you can connect the user with your business. Whether it's the sale of products online or simply a lead-generation tactic, the Web site will help you to bring your business closer to your clients. Think of it in the same way you would your offline advertising. The billboard advertisement brings the client to your store, and it's at this point that your sales force helps to close the deal. In the online world, your ads do the same thing, but now it's your Web site's job to close the deal for your business.

Developing a Winning Landing Page

When you're conducting any type of online campaign, whether it be a banner ad, newsletter promotion, or PPC campaign, you want to maximize the results of your effort. When done properly, a targeted landing page for an ad can greatly increase conversions, or the number of customers who act on your offer.

A landing page is a Web page created for the specific purpose of driving the target market toward some intended action based on the offer presented in an online ad. The action you want the target market to take might be to fill out a quote request form, a form to view a live online demo, or a form to download a white paper; to participate in a survey; or to purchase your products online. The key is that the landing page is geared toward racking up conversions—to convert browsers to buyers.

The way your landing page is developed depends entirely on your business objectives, your target market, and your products/services—sound familiar? A complex product or service likely will require a lead-generation form, whereas a simple product such as a book or vacation package would benefit from providing the target market with immediate access to the purchase process. The landing page should focus on only what needs to be present to get the conversion—keep it focused.

Tips for Creating Landing Page Content

Similar to any advertisement, creative copy plays a key role in the success of your communication strategy. The overall creative strategy and the copy presented on your landing page have a huge impact on the ability of the landing page to create the conversion. When preparing the copy for your landing page, keep the following tips in mind:

- Your landing page should repeat and expand on the offer. The job of your online advertisements is to generate interest in your offer, whereas the job of the landing page is to close the loop and create the conversion. The volume of content on your landing page depends entirely on what you are selling and the objective you are trying to accomplish. For example, if you are promoting a particular gift basket for Valentine's Day, then you will not need a lot of copy to close the sale; however, if you are selling an expensive, complex point-of-sale system, your target market will likely want to know additional details about the product.

- Your landing page should clearly define the benefits of your offer. The benefits the target market receives from the product or service you are promoting are what justifies the purchase.

- Your landing page should deliver on the promise made in your advertisement. If your ad was focused around getting the target market to sign up for an online demo, then when they follow through to the landing page they should be given the opportunity to do so. Do not send the target market on a wild goose hunt for the information or product offering they requested.

- Your landing page should speak to your target market. What tone, or personality, works best with your target market? If your offer was in the form of a newsletter, then the same style should extend to the landing page to create a natural linkage. Little things make a difference.

- Your landing page should have a captivating header statement. The header statement is what keeps the target market's interest piqued when they click through on your advertisement. You need to keep the momentum going. Repeating a variation of the headline of the advertisement often is quite effective, as it lets the users know that they are viewing exactly what the advertisement promised before the click-through.

- Your landing page should be easy to read, or better yet, skim. It is a well-known fact that your typical Internet user does not read all of the information on the page. People also tend to have more difficulty reading online than they do on print, so it takes them longer to review material. Knowing this, be sure to keep your content concise and to the point, as well as written at a grade level suitable for your entire target market.

- Your landing page content should minimize risk. If your target market hesitates, then you are likely to lose the sale. If you have a money-back guarantee, emphasize it! Anything that helps de-stress your target market and close the deal should be prominently displayed.

- Your landing page should promote the "value-added" portion of the offer that will help with your objectives. Free shipping, free gift with purchase, received coupon or discount toward a future purchase, the number of reward points earned with purchase, etc., all add to the value of the offer.

- Your landing page should create a sense of urgency. Asking the target market to "Act Now!" telling the target market that "there are limited quantities" or "limited space available," and techniques like time-stamping the offer with an expiry date create a sense of urgency that encourages the target market to take immediate advantage of the offer. If the target market does not feel as though there is a reason to act on an offer now, then your chances of converting them decrease significantly.

- Your landing page should include content that increases your credibility, such as client testimonials or product/service reviews. For example, a hotel that has a AAA 4 Diamond Rating can leverage its status on the landing page by including mention of it on the page; this could be as simple as including the logo on the landing page. Content that helps establish credibility also helps build trust, which is key to doing business online.

- Your landing page should ask for the sale. You presented the target market with an offer you want to capitalize on, so take advantage of that and ask for the sale. You put too much effort into getting them to your Web site. Make it absolutely clear what the next step is that you want the target market to take. An action button that says "register for your live demo now" is much more effective that a button that says "submit."

- Your landing page should be optimized for the search engines. If you are running a promotion for only a couple of days, the odds are that you do not want your landing page indexed by the search engines. In this case, you would use your robots' exclusion protocol in your robots.txt file to tell the search engines not to index the page. For the rest of you, optimizing your landing page for the major search engines is important. In fact, if the exact keyword phrase the target market searched for is found on your homepage, on average your conversions will be higher.

Be sure to take the time to work relevant keyword phrases into your landing page. With your pay-to-play campaigns, you can purchase a number of targeted phrases; but with the bidding prices for keywords on the rise, taking some of the pressure off with natural search engine listings can help generate additional sales through phrases you may not want to purchase and may increase your bottom line because you're benefiting from traffic you did not have to pay for. What have you got to lose?

You know your target market best and what information they want to know before making a purchase. When it comes down to it, your content should speak your target market's language, complete the pitch made in the ad, build trust, and close the sale. Test different lengths, tones, and formatting of copy to find the right balance to best sell your offer. Keep in mind that great content helps build trust, and it is trust that drives online sales and builds lifetime customer relationships.

Tips for Planning the Layout of Your Landing Page

So laying out a landing page is just like building a new page for your Web site, right? Wrong. Remember, you're bringing your prospective client to your offer; thus it is critical that all elements that are going to encourage the conversion be placed accordingly on the landing page. Consider the following tips when planning the layout for your landing pages:

- Keep the most important information above the fold. The fold is where the bottom of the browser window sits and additional scrolling is required to view the remaining content. For about half of the Internet population, the preferred screen resolution is 800 x 600; the majority of the remaining population uses a resolution that is higher. Standard practice is to include all information that is critical to the sale above the fold for a typical 800 x 600 user. On average, the higher that information rests on a page, the more important it is assumed to be.

- Be wary of "banner blindness." People have become so used to viewing Web pages with banner ads that run along the very top of the page that they naturally dismiss that area. Make sure you do not post any mission-critical information at the very top of the page, but if you do happen to do so, make sure it stands out. Likewise, people tend to ignore content that looks and smells like an ad in shape, size, and color. Be careful to avoid giving this impression with key content on your landing page.

- Watch out for triggers that cause the target market to lose interest or stop viewing. If your content runs more than a single page, make sure it is obvious that there is more to view. Avoid using line breaks and excessive white space to separate content, because this can give the target market the impression that they have viewed everything worthwhile.

- If your initial promotion went out in the form of a newsletter, then it is beneficial to extend the "look and feel" of the newsletter over to the landing page to maintain a bridge. The target market is familiar with your newsletter and you want to maintain that familiarity.

- Your landing page should eliminate anything that might distract the target market from their original goal. The last thing you want is for the target market to get distracted and wander off, disregarding the original offer. You should focus on what is necessary to close the sale, which means getting rid of excess clutter such as your Web site navigation. Your landing page could include a link back to the home page of your Web site so that your target market will have access to your full site. A common approach here is to make your company logo clickable. You can also include a link in the footer area of the landing page back to your home page.

- Subtly cross-promote features that will help you market your business in the future. You want to give the target market the option to sign up for your permission marketing–based newsletter and to make use of the viral marketing tell-a-friend function, but you do not want these elements to take over the page and distract the user. Careful placement and presentation of value-added calls to action can help you promote your business without taking away from the primary message.

- Include navigation options that give value to the target market. Your target market will want access to privacy information, security information, shipping information, warranty/returns/exchanges information, access to "help" content if there are likely to be questions, and contact information. Ensure that this information is readily accessible.

- Make good use of font types and styles, and color, as well as photography to sell your product or service offering. If photography is going to help sell your offer, make sure you use good-quality images. Images that look cheap extend to your offer as well, which may damage the ability of your landing page to successfully convert customers.

- Your landing page should prominently display alternative purchase/ registration options. In fact, anything you want the target market to act on needs to stand out. Your target might be extremely interested in your offer but not so enthused about making a purchase online, or your target might need a little help and may want to talk to someone. You can make your target market's life easier by making your phone number very visible on the page, along with posting additional contact information in the footer of the Web page, such as a customer service e-mail address, fax number, Web site address, and postal address.

- If the purpose of your landing page is to collect customer information, then you need to provide your target market with a reason, or incentive, to give you that information in order to increase your response rate. Reward your target market for taking the time to fill out your form with a free whitepaper, an option to join your newsletter, a discount off a future purchase, or the like. The incentive has to relate directly to what you are asking of the target market.

- Make the actual purchase process or registration form as simple as possible. People like things that are clear and easy to understand. If you have a registration form for a downloadable demo on your landing page, be sure you only ask the questions you need at the time. You do not need the target market's mailing address at this stage; it only complicates the matter, which decreases the chances of the individual's completing the form. I remember hearing somewhere that for every additional step or question asked that does not pertain directly to the target market's initial intent, you lose 10 percent of your audience.

In line with keeping the buying/registration process as simple as possible, make sure you always downplay the effort involved to complete the transaction. For example, if you have a registration form that spans two pages, then offer visual cues such as "Step 1 of 2" so that the target market knows what to expect at all times.

- All of the best practices techniques that go into building a Web site apply to your landing page as well. The landing page still has to be cross-browser-compatible, be easy to use, be quick to load, have clean code, and effectively brand your business, etc.

Arming yourself with the right message and the right presentation of the message is essential to making your landing page work for you. If you simply put together your landing pages with little or no thought, you truly defeat the purpose of the technique. Similar to your Web site and online marketing strategy development, take the time and do it right the first time.

Proper Landing Page Execution

Now that you know what is critical to designing a proper landing page, it's time to focus on the actual execution of your landing pages—meaning, how you actually build the pages and what's appropriate for your business. What is the right approach for your business? Well, as always, that relates specifically back to the foundation of your online marketing initiatives. Consider the following when determining what approach is relevant to your business:

- Do you have a lot to say about the product or service that you are offering to your clients? If your landing page reads like ancient scrolls and runs on for pages and pages in length, it is recommended that you consider two things:

  - Do you really need all that content? If it is not critical to the offer, you should consider discarding it.

  - If all of the content is necessary to selling your product or service, then expanding the landing page into a mini-site made up of a few pages is worth consideration.

Just like a landing page, the mini-site should be solely focused on the single offer you are promoting; however, the pages within can be allocated to address the specific content you need across logical categories. As a high-level example, your mini-site might contain comprehensive product information that covers different variations of the offering on individual pages, a features-comparison page, access to a demo, a frequently asked questions page, and a quote request page. The structure of your mini-site depends entirely on the offer you are promoting.

- In some cases you may not need a landing page at all. For example, if you are introducing a new clothing line, it is probably not cost-effective to develop individual landing pages for each article of clothing. Instead, you would be more apt to include the new clothing line on your Web site. You would use your newsletter to promote the clothing line and include links directly to the articles of clothing within your online storefront or catalogue, where the target market can make the purchase on the spot.

J.Crew is a good example of a retailer that uses the Internet to promote and sell its products. Figure 5.5 is a screenshot of a recent e-mail promotion they sent out to subscribers:

The e-mail promotion presents a number of product offers to the target market. Clicking on any product takes the target market directly to the

Figure 5.5. A sample e-mail promotion used by J.Crew to drive users to make online purchases.

page on the J.Crew Web site where he or she could purchase the selection (see Figure 5.6). The entire process is very simple.

This approach works well for standardized products that can be sold in bulk quantities, such as clothing, books, DVDs, crafts, chocolates, gift baskets, boxed software, and video games, and the list goes on and on. With these articles the target market is generally sold before they come to your site; they are looking to simply make the purchase. When they get to your Web site, you might offer them a few different alternatives, such as different color sweaters or different options for a Valentine's Day gift basket, but not a lot of explaining needs to be done to sell the product—the target market knows what they're getting and they just want to buy it.

- Depending on your business, it might be necessary to have landing pages that speak to different market segments—demographic, geographic, and psychographic. For example, if you are doing business internationally, language and cultural considerations come into play. The English page that worked for your market in the United States will not work for your market in China. You need to tailor your landing pages to speak directly to your target market segments.

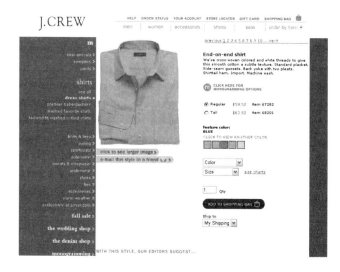

Figure 5.6. J.Crew takes users directly to the product specific page where the buying process begins.

- If you can personalize your landing page with customer information you have on record, you should do so. Anything you can do to make the experience more pleasant and the purchase/request process easier for your target should be taken into consideration.

  For example, you might have a welcome message aimed directly at the individual who clicks through to the landing page, or you might pull known information from your customer database to automatically populate fields of the order form such as the customer's name, shipping address, and credit card information. In this case, all the buyer has to do is review the order and hit the "buy" button to complete the process—quick and simple.

  If you are running an affiliate program, you might look at carrying a level of personalization over from the affiliate Web site to your landing page. The target market was browsing your affiliate's Web site, took an interest in your offering, and clicked through to give you an opportunity to seal the deal. If the target market hits your landing page and sees a message stating "as seen on. . . ," they are able to link the relationship between your business and the affiliate, which can help you get the sale.

  The level of personalization you employ depends entirely on your budget, objectives, and current business systems. The personalization functionality might be driven dynamically by your content management tool, CRM package, or affiliate program. If you are sending out an e-mail promotion, then ideally the promotion would be tagged to individual customer accounts to dynamically create customized landing pages when the target market clicks through.

- Be sure to leave your landing page accessible well after the fact. Because a landing page is built around a specific offer, it typically has a limited intended lifespan. The landing page will be useful for you until the offer has ended.

  It is important to understand that online offers tend to have a good half life. A friend might pass a newsletter on to another friend who passes it on to another friend and so forth. You may have people trickling to your landing page through the offer well past the intended run. Rather than present them with an error page saying the page no longer exists, it is best to leave the page active if you have no qualms about accepting business based on the offer in the future. You may leave the landing page up for several weeks or a few months, depending on the typical lifespan of your campaigns.

If the campaign has a limited lifespan and the offer cannot extend over a period of time, then be sure to leave a message on the landing page to explain that the offer is over and direct them to other opportunities that they might have an interest in. Always make the best of every opportunity.

- It is not just about having the right landing page. What you do to follow up after the target market makes a purchase or submits a request reflects directly on how the customer perceives your business. You want your customers to feel appreciated and to trust you so that they continue to be your customers in the future.

When your target market completes the action on your landing page, make sure you have a "Thank You" page that displays following completion of the process. This thank you page might thank the customers for their interest or purchase, offer them contact information should they want to reach you, and include any other pertinent information such as details on how to track their purchase. If it makes sense to do so for your business, you might also send out an e-mail receipt or confirmation to the target market.

If the purpose of your landing page was to collect leads, then follow up with a phone call, e-mail, or mailer immediately while your lead is hot!

If you design your landing page in line with your target market's expectations, ask them to take a specific action, and make it easy for them to do so, you should see great success with your landing pages. Perhaps you find you are getting a lot of click-throughs, but your sales are disappointing. This is likely because your landing page is not up to par, which is why it is so important to monitor your results, continually test your pages, and make improvements over time. Remember, it's important to monitor all of your online marketing activities so you can ensure that you maximize the effectiveness of all of your campaigns.

Making PPC Campaigns Work for You

PPC advertising, or Pay per Click, has become an essential part of every business's online marketing strategy. If you're reading this book we are assuming you know what PPC advertising channel is, but for those who may not, these advertising channels enable businesses to pay for exposure in search engine results or on various content sites based on targeted keywords and phrases.

Why is PPC advertising so popular? Well, there is a pretty easy answer to that question. PPC advertising enables businesses to put their products or services in front of their target market at a fraction of the cost of traditional advertising, which will bring your business a higher return on investment and an increased customer base. Google AdWords (see Figure 5.7), Yahoo! Search Marketing Solutions (see Figure 5.8), and MSN adCenter (see Figure 5.9) are today's more popular PPC advertising models. Just think of it like this. You could pay a hefty fee to place a two-page ad in a targeted trade publication, but you always run the risk that the ad will generate a low response rate—if any. That has always been the gamble.

Instead, PPC advertising enables you to pay only for the number of times your ad is clicked on by your target market—not the number of times your ad is viewed or displayed. What this results in is targeted exposure for your business. If you implement your campaigns the right way, your return on investment should be significantly higher than that of traditional advertising campaigns; you just need to make sure all the tools are in place to create the conversion.

The most important thing to remember when setting up your PPC campaigns is the fact that taking the time to do it right can mean a world of difference between success and failure. Just like everything else mentioned

Figure 5.7. The Google AdWords PPC channel (*http://adwords.google.com*).

Figure 5.8.   The Yahoo! Search Marketing Solutions PPC channel (*http://searchmarketing.yahoo.com*).

Figure 5.9.   MSN's new adCenter PPC channel (*http://adcenter.msn.com*).

throughout this book, it is critical that you take the foundation of your Internet marketing strategy into consideration prior to launching your PPC campaigns. Yes, Google AdWords boasts that you can setup your advertising account and begin advertising in less than 20 minutes. Trust me, if you are not an experienced PPC advertiser, this is not the best approach to take. Take the time, plan your strategy, and do it right the first time.

Strategically Select Your Keywords

When planning your PPC strategies, start by revisiting the foundation for your entire Web site strategy. Who is your target market? What are you promoting? What is the perceived value that your product or service offers? What behavioral patterns does your target market typically follow during the buying process for your product or service? These are all questions that will help you.

It is important to understand that pinpointing how consumers are going to search for your products or services is very difficult to forecast. An understanding of your environment and how your customers perceive your business is the first step. How have past customers found your business? What calls to action and benefit statements have your customers responded to from past campaigns? Review your traffic logs and see what keywords users have used to find your site. Analyze your competition to see what they are using. Ultimately you will develop a great list of keyword candidates. This is a good start, but remember that your perceived expectations of what your consumers respond to versus what they will actually use when searching for your products and services are dramatically different.

There are also a number of subscription services that are available to help you select appropriate keywords for your PPC campaigns. These services base their suggestions on results from actual search queries. Wordtracker *(http://www.wordtracker.com/)* is a great example of a keyword tool that is available in the marketplace (see Figure 5.10). WordTracker maintains a database of over 350 million keywords sourced from several meta search engines. The tool is easy to use and provides a valuable source of information. When you run a search for a term, it will show you related keywords, including misspellings, the plural and singular versions of the word or phrase, and references from its thesaurus if desired.

For in-depth strategies and tactics to identify keywords and phrases for your PPC strategy, it is recommended that you reference *101 Ways to Promote Your Web Site*, the complementary book to *3G Marketing on the Internet*.

Remember, you will never have the perfect list at the beginning of your campaign. Just like the implementation of all other online marketing campaigns, your PPC strategy will require that you implement and continuously monitor and refine your strategy until it is optimized for performance. You should always start off with a lengthy list of keywords to test the waters with your PPC program of choice. What is working and what is converting? You'll be able to learn quickly if you stay on top of campaign activity on a daily basis. Eventually you'll be able to filter down your list to a sample of keywords that are proven to convert for your business.

Figure 5.10. The Wordtracker keyword research tool (*http://www.wordtracker.com*).

It's easy to get carried away with your PPC campaigns as well. Quite often a company will monitor its keywords and notice that certain keywords are generating a lot of exposure (not thinking about conversions) and will take the next step and set up advanced broad phrase matches for the different keywords and phrases with the hope of catching additional exposure. Businesses almost immediately notice an increase in the amount of traffic that is generated as a result of these campaign efforts. Sounds good, doesn't it? What you need to realize is that this is a quick way to blow through your online marketing budget. Instead, focus on targeted keywords that are going to convert. If you use a standard-match keyword or phrase that converts consistently, wouldn't you rather capture the majority of users searching using these particular search criteria, as opposed to those using the broad match that will use the majority of your budget but will provide little return on investment? Spend your marketing budget wisely. It's easy to get carried away.

Understand Your Customers

The more you know about your customers and how they will react to your ads, the more you can maximize your PPC strategy. If you write ads that will speak to your customers directly, but will let window shoppers who are not interested in your products or services (and those who will not convert) know that this offer is not for them, you will attract only qualified prospects to your Web site. This also enables you to reduce wasted clicks, thus maximizing your budget.

Like any campaign, it's critical that you monitor what your customers are responding to. Simply changing one word in a PPC ad could result in increased click-throughs for your business. When setting up your PPC ads, you are limited to what you can say to your customers to bring them to the front door. It's important that your ads relate specifically to the keywords they are associated with and make sure your message is clear. When a user views one of your ads, you want that user to know that this is exactly what he or she is looking for. This will ensure that your clicks are targeted and that you minimize the amount of unqualified clicks that you receive.

Don't Use Your Budget So Quickly

Many advertisers assume that they need to bid into the top-tier positions of the PPC ad network to make their PPC strategy work for their company. Bidding into the top positions for more competitive keywords will generate increased exposure for your business, but it will also help you to blow through your budget more quickly. When creating the strategy for your PPC campaigns, you should develop a strategy to maximize both your daily budget and the exposure for your business.

If your ads were appearing within the lower ranks, you could receive just as much exposure for a lower CPC (cost per click), resulting in more exposure for your business as a whole. Maximize your PPC budget by bidding into the lower ranks to minimize your average CPC. This will enable you to maximize the length of time that your ads are in rotation on the PPC network during a given day while maximizing your PPC advertising budget.

In addition, when you are performing your keyword research for your PPC campaigns, you should drill deep to identify those keywords that are proven to be effective, but are not being utilized by your competition. These are the words that can help you to drive targeted traffic to your Web site, but will have a minimal CPC as nobody else is sponsoring these words. Nine times out of 10, advertisers focus on the most popular keywords, which are also the words that have a higher CPC. This strategy will help you steer clear of this budget strainer.

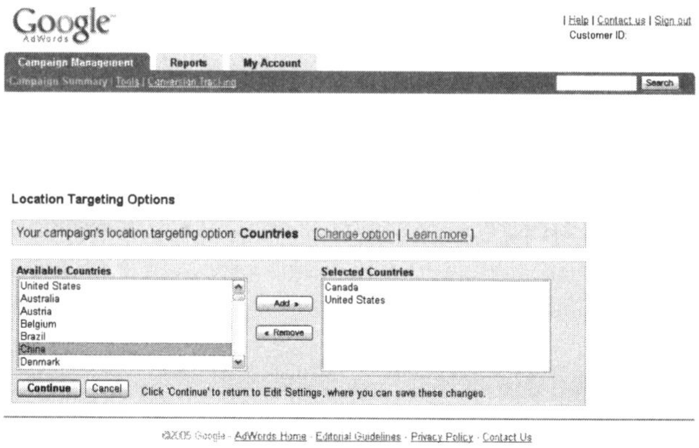

Figure 5.11. Geo targeting PPC campaigns with Google AdWords.

Geo-Targeting Your Campaigns

When analyzing your sales records and your traffic logs, monitor where your business is coming from to see if you notice any trends. Many PPC advertising networks enable you to target where your ads are displayed based on your target market's geographic location (see Figure 5.11). Having said this, if you notice that a particular amount of your business is coming from one specific geographic location, you can target this location to attempt to capitalize on this trend. With today's technology, you can target users by country, state, or even city. By ensuring that you target only those locations where you wish your ads to appear, you maximize your online advertising dollars, whether you are working with a small or a large budget.

Use Landing Pages

We've already discussed the importance of using landing pages, but we cannot stress enough how important it is to ensure that you follow through on the offer directly from your PPC ads. It's critical that the page users are directed to when they click on your ad provides the users with information about what you are promoting. Without doing so, your return on your investment will be minimal, which equals one thing—no conversions. More details on how to develop winning landing pages, can be found earlier in this chapter.

Target Your Customers by Dayparting

Staying on top of your campaign performance can benefit your business in more ways than one. When analyzing your traffic logs and PPC conversion ratios, you'll more than likely notice what time of day and what day of the week users are more apt to click on your ads and when they convert into paying customers. If you notice a significant increase in your click-through rates at a specific time, you can capitalize on this increased visibility. Through understanding this information, you can adjust your PPC strategy to capitalize on this behavior.

This strategy requires in-depth analysis of conversion rates, click-through rates, and general traffic levels. Having said that, the basic premise behind dayparting is that you as an advertiser can increase your conversions during the time of day when users will be most apt to view information on your products or services. During this high-exposure timeframe, you can increase your CPC to ensure that you are maximizing your exposure on the different PPC networks to your target market. By doing so, and ensuring that all of the other tools are in place (e.g., proper ads, landing pages, etc.), you will capitalize on the increased exposure and ultimately will convert more prospects to customers.

Getting Noticed in the World of Spam

With an increased amount of e-mail marketing taking place in today's marketplace, getting noticed by your customers is proving to be more difficult every day. According to eMarketer, the volume of e-mail in the United States alone is projected to double from 1.5 trillion in 2003 to 2.7 trillion in 2007. With this high volume of messages being distributed by marketers, it is important not only that your messages are delivered to your clients, but also that your messages are designed appropriately to encourage your users to respond to those messages.

Why would you have a problem getting your messages to your clients, you might ask? Well, according to a study by Pivotal Veracity, between January 25 and February 25, 2005, approximately 84.4 percent of all messages delivered by marketers actually landed in the recipient's inbox. An additional 5.6 percent of the messages ended up in the users' bulk mail folder. What happened to the other 10.0 percent of messages, you might ask? Well, they never even made it to the user; they're classified as "missing." We'll explain how this happens shortly, but the study also noted a few other very interesting statistics and key lessons:

- Nine out of every 10 HTML messages that are distributed by marketers are not W3C HTML compliant. This results in HTML rendering issues—mostly in popular e-mail programs such as MSN, Hotmail, and GMail. In addition, many delivery issues can be directly attributed to poor design and development of HTML messages.

- Not all ISPs actually distribute bounce-backs to inform the marketer that the message was blocked or was not delivered. Many ISPs simply delete the messages. From an ISP's perspective, it's important to understand that with the volume of messages that are being delivered on a daily basis, it is difficult to accommodate the needs of marketers—all the reason for us to try harder to ensure that our messages get to our subscribers.

With an increase in the amount of spam that is being distributed online, there are more and more factors coming into play to prevent Internet users from being bombarded with unsolicited promotions. These same prevention measures are also making it more difficult for marketers to communicate with their opt-in subscriber list via e-mail. Remember, having permission to send your clients e-mail promotions is the first step, but you also need to focus on actually getting the messages to them.

To understand the different factors that could prevent you from delivering messages to your clients, consider the points below.

- *ISP Prevention Measures:* Probably one of the most common prevention techniques that is being implemented today is that ISPs are now maintaining blacklists on their servers. A blacklist is a list of IP addresses that the ISP denies any incoming connections. In other words, if you're sending a message to an ISP that has your IP address on a blacklist, you're not going to be able to get past the gate to get your messages to the intended recipients.

- *Distributed and ISP Content Filters:* Today there are several organizations helping both ISPs and businesses to deal with their spam problems. Content filters help organizations to filter incoming messages based on common characteristics of spam messages. If the content filters identify a red flag in an incoming message, they will prevent the message from reaching the intended recipient.

- *Publicly Accessible Blacklists:* There are many publicly accessible black-lists and whitelists that are often used by smaller ISPs and businesses that do not have a dedicated e-mail administrator to monitor incoming messages. As explained earlier, a blacklist is a list of known offenders; however, a whitelist is the complete opposite. The organizations listed on a whitelist are viewed as bonded e-mail marketers—meaning businesses that follow best practices to obtain information and ensure that all recipients have requested to receive their e-mail promotions. Blacklists that are widely used by businesses today include SpamCop (see Figure 5.12), Mail Abuse Prevention System, and Spam Prevention Early Warning System.

- *User-Level Content Filters:* Today, more and more Internet users have anti-spam software programs set up on their computers to help fight against spam messages. In fact, almost every e-mail client available today provides a junk mail filter of some sort. The effectiveness of the different tools varies; however, the one thing that is clear is that you, as a marketer, have to try even harder to get your messages through to your subscribers.

- *User-Driven Blacklists and Whitelists:* Many popular e-mail applications that are widely used by Internet users (e.g., AOL, MSN, Yahoo! and even Microsoft Outlook) enable users to build their own black-lists and whitelists to manage spam messages. Also, there are a number of challenge response systems available that will distribute a message

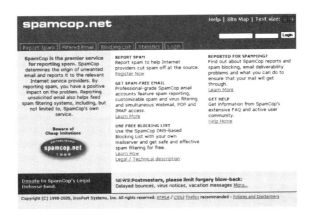

Figure 5.12. SpamCop is one of the top services for reporting spam on the Internet.

to non-whitelisted senders to confirm their authenticity and purpose by entering a provided code into their system prior to the message being delivered.

Key for you to understand: Sending messages is not as simple as an e-mail going from your computer to your customers. There are various obstacles between points A and B that you need to pass before you even get to the inbox. It's for this reason that you need to take the time to plan your campaigns appropriately, work with a quality opt-in database, work with the best delivery and tracking tools available, and design your campaigns to achieve your online marketing objectives.

In-house Versus Outsource E-mail Marketing

Ensuring that you're working with the right tools to build your opt-in list, launch your campaigns, and track your results is just as important as what you're saying to your customers. Without selecting the right tools to work with, you run the risk of not even getting your messages to your clients, as just noted. There are three basic choices that you have to work with when planning your e-mail marketing strategy, which include:

1. *In-House (Licensed Software):* Enables you to perform all the marketing services and technical services with internal resources; license the software; and host the application on your own servers.

2. *Outsource (Application Service Provider, or ASP):* Utilize a Web-based e-mail application to manage your contact database, distribute e-mails, and track distribution and response metrics.

3. *Outsource (Marketing Service Provider):* These full-service agreements provide for outsourcing of both the technical and marketing activities.

With today's complex e-mail marketing environment—particularly when dealing with all of the deliverability issues that are present in today's marketplace—it is recommended that you choose the ASP model, as it simply makes the most sense for most organizations. The functional and technical requirements of an e-mail marketing program tend to be similar across many organizations, and therefore a provider that focuses on those services can deliver them at a superior level with lower overall costs. What are the challenges that you face when going with either an in-house or an outsourced solution? Consider the following:

In-House E-mail Marketing Challenges

- *Software Selection:* Picking a technology that is compatible with your internal CRM systems and network configuration.

- *IT Resources:* Do you have personnel to manage the application, provide system modifications, and assist with delivery issues, software upgrades, off-hours support, etc.?

- *E-mail Distribution:* Scalability along with the ability to regulate the speed of sending messages to your opt-in database.

- *Bounce Handling:* The ability to manage the traffic that comes back as a result of e-mail replies and bounces.

- *E-mail Deliverability:* Blacklisting, whitelisting, spam filters, spam complaints, ongoing resources to test deliverability.

- *Security:* Ensuring that your list is not easily accessible to potential hackers.

- *Data Management:* Integration of data between multiple internal systems and software applications.

- *Financial Resources:* The budget associated with the purchase, license, and setup of the software, as well as periodic upgrades. ASP agreements allow for the expenditure to be listed as an expense and to be paid for over time.

Outsource Challenges

- *Expertise:* Selecting a vendor that has the experience and staff to handle the same issues that you would face internally.

- *Security:* Selecting a vendor that follows best practices in the hosting and e-mail marketing disciplines.

- *Data Integration:* Selecting a vendor that can provide custom-integrated solutions to easily migrate data between internal systems and your external e-mail database.

- *Focus:* Selecting a vendor that specializes in the services you need. For example, marketing services often are best provided internally by the marketing department or through an arrangement with a marketing agency that is in tune with the marketing strategies of the organization. E-mail marketing is no longer a disjointed effort, but rather an important element of the marketing mix. In many cases, the organization simply needs the assistance of an Application Service Provider to execute on the technical components of your e-mail marketing campaign.

Just because we are recommending the ASP model, we are not saying that you should choose just any ASP to work with. *Be very careful with your decision-making process.* You're talking about the future of your company's e-mail marketing endeavors here, so it's critical that the solution you select meets all of your requirements, will get your messages to your users, and will enable you to learn about your customers so that you can serve your customers better.

Working With the Right Tools

There are a number of different things that you should be looking for when determining which e-mail marketing program is right for your business. With e-mail marketing becoming a staple component of many online marketing strategies, the number of e-mail marketing tools available in the marketplace is growing rapidly. How different are all of the ASP tools that are available? Well, there are a number of great e-mail marketing tools out there, all of which offer similar features and measurement tools. So if there are so many options available that all offer the same features, why does it matter which one you choose?

We asked ourselves that very same question one day and embarked on a journey to evaluate several tools that were considered to be leaders in the marketplace. This wasn't solely for our own benefit. We wanted to find a tool that we were comfortable recommending to our clients and that would ensure that each of our client's campaigns were as effective as possible. On top of reviewing the functionality of each of these tools, we also spent a significant amount of time querying vendors about various items that fall outside of the core functionality of their tools. This is where you can distinguish one organization from another. Simply asking the question "what does your organization do to ensure that my messages get delivered to my clients?" is a great starting point. Typically, most organizations have a canned response to this question. Something like "well, we abide by the privacy laws" or, my favorite, "our tool uses the most current technology to ensure all of your messages are delivered to their intended recipients."

The reality of the Internet is the fact that all messages distributed during a given campaign will not be delivered. Soft bounces, hard bounces, and invalid addresses—this is the nature of the Internet. Abiding by privacy laws and following best practice standards for data collection are a must for any business looking to launch an effective e-mail marketing campaign. What about blacklists, content filters, and actually monitoring bounced e-mail when you launch a campaign? These were all questions that were raised during our analysis, and it was no surprise that many of the "industry leaders" didn't know how to answer them.

The good news is that a handful of e-mail marketing programs are being offered in the marketplace that scored a winning grade during our analysis. Take the nTarget (*http://www.ntarget.com*) e-mail marketing system that has been developed by Intercerve, Inc, a software development company based in North Carolina. The nTarget system (see Figure 5.13) was first developed in 1998, which immediately told us that this wasn't a typical "fly by night" organization that was simply trying to capitalize on the popularity of e-mail marketing. They've been around for a while, and this was clear from the moment we first spoke to their team. In fact, many of the questions that were raised to suppliers during our analysis didn't even come up as this organization understood the industry, the state of the Internet, and what a company requires to launch a successful campaign.

What distinguished this organization from other suppliers that were interviewed was their commitment not only to continuously improving their technology, but also to developing strong relationships with leading ISPs in the marketplace. For example, earlier in this chapter we reviewed all of the

Figure 5.13. nTarget is truly a "best of breed" e-mail marketing solutions (*http://www.ntarget.com*).

potential barriers that could prevent your messages from being delivered to your clients. Well, an example of what nTarget is doing to ensure that your messages get delivered to your clients is that they are on what is referred to as an "enhanced whitelist" with AOL. For the record, there are not a lot of e-mail marketing suppliers that can have their IP address included on this list. Why is nTarget on the list? It's because they are committed to following the highest best practice standards of e-mail marketing and are one of the leaders in the anti-spam movement that is sweeping across the Internet. No campaign is launched from the nTarget system unless the recipient has opted in to receive information from the vendor, and this is something that nTarget works diligently to promote to ISPs around the globe to ensure the highest deliverability rates possible for their clients.

What about user-level content filters? A staple component of the nTarget system is its built-in spam checker (see Figure 5.14). Before you launch any campaign with their system, you can run your promotion through the spam checker to identify any red flags in your promotion that could trigger a content filter to assume you're sending spam (see Figure 5.14). This is a feature that is available in numerous e-mail marketing tools; however, this feature, combined with nTarget's commitment to developing strong relationships at the ISP level, immediately impressed us.

Figure 5.14.   nTarget (*http://www.ntarget.com*) has a built in spam checker.

Other key features and highlights of the nTarget e-mail marketing solution include:

- *Managing Bouncebacks:* When you launch an e-mail marketing campaign with the nTarget system, the tool itself will process all non-delivery receipts (NDR), which most people refer to as "bounced" e-mail messages. nTarget's integrated NDR system evaluates all returned e-mail messages to determine whether they should be processed automatically or forwarded to the administrator for review. E-mail addresses that generate an NDR are evaluated over several promotion runs, depending on the type of return message, to determine whether the address is deactivated or remains as an active contact.

  In general, an NDR message is categorized according to what is happening at the other end of the e-mail transmission. For example, the NDR code 550 is translated as an invalid mailbox or host—this is usually what happens when the e-mail address is not valid or has been deactivated. This is what the industry refers to as a "hard bounce." A code 554 results when there is a failure in transmission or service—a hiccup on the Internet. A full mailbox will give you the code 552. Both codes 554 and 552 are referred to as "soft bounces" because of the higher possibility of being able to eventually deliver these messages to the user. We're explaining all of this because the nTarget solution manages all of this for you—something that most ASP solutions and definitely in-house software programs are lacking.

- *Campaign Tracking:* The nTarget e-mail marketing solution provides marketers with real-time reports to let you see how your campaigns are performing. The built-in reporting system tracks your total e-mails sent, any NDRs generated by the system, removal requests, your total click-throughs on each campaign, unique click-throughs, and any messages that have been forwarded by the user. The system tracks all links that are embedded within each of your promotions (both text links and image links) and will provide you with feedback on which content your clients are actually looking at. By monitoring user behavior, you can assign segmentation variables to users and send specific segments of your database specific promotions based on the behavioral patterns that they exhibit within your tracking.

- *Double Opt-In Application:* Following best practice industry standards, the nTarget system utilizes a double opt-in process to ensure that all subscribers are added to the opt-in database appropriately. When someone subscribes to a list that is powered by the nTarget system, a confirmation message is automatically sent to all e-mail addresses. When subscribers receive the e-mail message they must click on an embedded link or reply with "OK" to confirm they are in fact the owner of that e-mail address and wish to receive e-mail messages (see Figure 5.15). This is how the nTarget system ensures that all e-mail addresses within the database have actually opted in to receive promotions; thus, flagging promotions as spam is avoided.

Following this process has several advantages, including:

– Easier list administration

– Greater ROI (return on investment)

– Improved list quality, leading to higher response rates

– Less chance of an e-mail's being ignored as "spam"

– Safeguard against being "blacklisted" by various anti-spam organizations

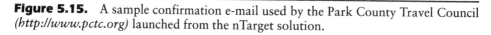

Figure 5.15. A sample confirmation e-mail used by the Park County Travel Council *(http://www.pctc.org)* launched from the nTarget solution.

– Safeguarding of your company's reputation by avoiding being labeled, sued, or penalized as a spammer.

- *WYSIWYG E-mail Editor:* The nTarget system provides users with an advanced e-mail editor that enables users to (1) develop HTML/text messages directly within the system, (2) import HTML code/text from an existing development program (e.g., Dreamweaver, notepad), or (3) edit existing promotions using the advanced WYSIWYG e-mail editing tool (see Figure 5.16). This makes developing your promotions and making last-minute revisions easy for marketers to perform. In a deadline-driven industry, any way that a marketer can save time is a good thing. This is a great feature included in the nTarget ASP application that helped to distinguish it from others involved in our analysis.

There are a number of great ASP e-mail marketing programs available that you can use to launch a successful e-mail marketing program for your business. The most important thing to keep in mind when evaluating your options is that you should look beyond the actual technology that the supplier is providing. Dig deeper to identify the supplier's reputation in the in-

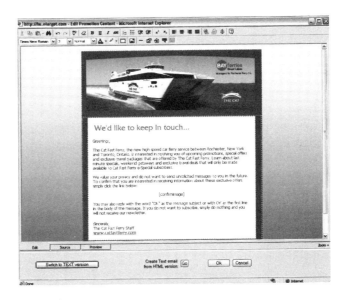

Figure 5.16. nTarget utilizes a built in WYSIWYG editor for quick and easy campaign edits.

dustry and how they are viewed by ISPs. You might be surprised what you find out. When conducting our analysis, it was surprising for us to find out that a popular ASP marketing program that is used by many businesses is actually on several blacklists; this does nothing for their clients, but if we didn't do our research, our clients potentially could have ended up with a poor supplier as well. Ask the right questions—it will pay off in the long run.

Designing Effective E-mail Promotions

So now that we know how important it is to work with the right e-mail marketing tools and how challenging it can be to actually get your messages to your customers, what exactly does it take to get your customers to respond to your message? Like the design of an effective landing page, a Web site, or even a print advertisement, there are several rules of thumb that should be followed when designing your e-mail promotions.

- *Leverage Your Brand:* Be sure to use your brand in the "from" line and your subject line of your e-mail promotions. This is critical as it could mean the difference between your customer's actually reading your message or not. By knowing who is sending the message and what the message actually contains, the recipient will see the messages as coming from a reliable source. This rule should be followed at all times.

- *Content Is Key:* Make sure that the content within your e-mail promotions is useful to the reader. Your subscribers signed up to receive your newsletter for a reason—you promised them something that was of interest to them. Make sure you follow through on that promise. Don't overwhelm the user with reams of content within your newsletter. Instead, present users with tidbits of information that they can visit your Web site to learn more about if it interests them. Your e-mail promotions should make the users feel good about the fact that they subscribed to receive your promotions. They should feel like they are getting something out if it.

- *Presentation Matters:* Having great content is one thing, but making sure users read it is another. Just like in a traditional direct-mail piece, bold font is a great way to emphasize a headline or a key takeaway from a paragraph of text. Try to avoid using underlined or italicized text in your e-mail promotions—they don't translate well and often are harder for the user to read.

Avoid developing e-mail promotions that contain paragraph after paragraph of content. Instead, use smaller paragraphs of content with clear calls to action that will direct the user to your Web site where he or she can view more content (see Figure 5.17). Let the design of your e-mail template facilitate an easy read as well. The use of shadow boxes, sidebars, and imagery can help to break up content to the point that it will not overwhelm the user.

Just like the presentation of content on a Web site, the use of bullets is a great way to get your message to your recipient without requiring the user to spend a significant amount of time reading your message. Using bullets enables you to highlight specific offers more clearly, it makes digesting the content in your newsletter much easier, and it also facilitates more of an overall user-friendly layout for your campaigns.

- *Clickable Graphics:* Make the graphics within your e-mail promotion clickable (see Figure 5.18). The more options that are included within your e-mail promotion for a user to click on, the higher the likelihood that you will get your customer to your site. Having said that, make sure that you point your users to the appropriate pages of your Web site or landing pages. Don't just send them to your home page if the graphic they click on promises something else. Give them what they want.

Figure 5.17. A sample e-mail promotion balancing short copy with image-based calls to action.

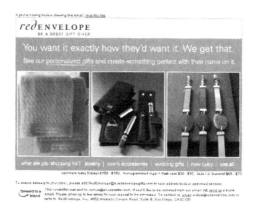

Figure 5.18. Sample campaigns used by RedEnvelope (*http://www.redenvelope.com*).

- *Captivate the User with Your Headline:* Just like in the print world, the headlines of your e-mail promotions should jump off the screen at your users. Use bold font in your headlines to make sure they stand out. Like designing a Web site, you want to ensure that the fonts you use in your promotions can actually be viewed by the recipient. Since many e-mail programs display default font styles (just like an Internet browser), you should stick with the tried and true fonts—Arial and Times New Roman.

- *Learn from Your Customers:* It's critical that you continuously learn from your customers, both when they sign up to receive your e-mail promotions and from the behavior that they exhibit when you're campaigning to them. For example, you can ask your users a few basic questions on your newsletter subscription form to help determine what each is interested in. The point is that the more you know about your customers, the more you can tailor each promotion to the user's specific needs.

- *Landing Pages:* We've already reviewed how critical the right landing page can be to your online marketing campaigns. Make sure that whatever it is you're promoting through your e-mail marketing campaigns, you send users to the offer and not to an unrelated page on your Web site. If you're promoting a number of different offers in a single campaign, take the time to create different landing pages for each offer. It will be worth it when you see an increase in your conversions from prospects to buyers.

- *Ask for the Sale:* Use calls to action wherever possible in your e-mail promotions. You're not campaigning to users simply to let them know that you're still around. You want to generate repeat business for your company. If you're telling users about a featured promotion, ask them to purchase your product. Don't simply highlight the promotion and hope that the users click on a link to visit your site to make the purchase. Ask them to do it with clear calls to action.

Integrating Your Strategy

When implementing your online marketing strategy, every business typically shares two common objectives: (1) customer acquisition and (2) customer retention. Whether you are launching PPC advertising campaigns, implementing e-mail marketing, or executing an offline postcard campaign, it is critical that you integrate your online and offline marketing efforts to acquire and retain your customer base. At a minimum, new Web site visitors should opt in to receive future correspondence from your business. By doing so, you will be provided with the opportunity to learn more about your prospects, customize future promotions to their unique interests, and ultimately convert prospective customers to buyers.

Consider the following illustration in Figure 5.19:

As you can see, regardless of how you are promoting your Web site— whether it be through PPC campaigns, newspaper advertisements, or simply

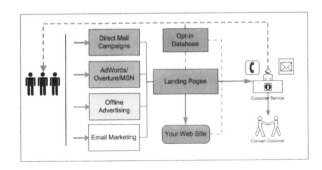

Figure 5.19.   Integrating your online and offline marketing efforts to maximize campaign effectiveness.

word-of-mouth marketing—once a user enters your Web site, he or she should either (1) sign up for your newsletter (at a minimum) or (2) convert from a prospect to a customer. The latter option should walk the user through the online purchase process while capturing permission from the user to communicate with him or her on a regular basis via targeted e-mail communication. From this point forward, it is a continuous process of learning more about both the prospects and the customers that are in your opt-in database. The more you learn, the better you can target your promotions to these individuals. Ultimately this will result in greater customer retention, increased sales, and a stronger overall loyalty to your brand.

Remember, your customers don't want to be annoyed when you send them e-mail promotions. They have opted in because they see value in the promise that you made when you asked them to sign up for your e-mail promotions. Take the time to understand what they are interested in and give them what they want. Don't hammer them with promotions containing information that they have no interest in whatsoever. If you do, the quality and value of your list will decrease quickly.

Building Your Opt-in Database

Building your opt-in database should be one of your top priorities when developing your online marketing strategy. But how do you build your list? Well, first of all you need to determine what data you currently have that you can use. With today's privacy laws, it's important to remember that you can't simply use your customer database to start launching opt-in campaigns. Just because people have provided you with their e-mail address when they purchased a product from you doesn't mean that you can feel free to send them promotions at your convenience. This goes against the essence of opt-in marketing.

So how do you get permission to send e-mail promotions to these individuals? Spend some time putting together an opt-in consent e-mail message that you can distribute to your database of customers. The objective of this message is simple—let your customers know that you're interested in staying in touch with them. It's critical that you explain why you want to do so. Let users know what is in it for them to sign up. Figure 5.20 shows an example of an opt-in consent newsletter that was distributed by Bay Ferries, Great Lakes (*www.catfastferry.com*)—the ferry service that runs between Toronto (Ontario) and Rochester (New York). The objective of the message was to let users know that the organization wanted to stay in touch to keep people informed about upcoming promotions, last-minute travel specials, contests, etc. Users could either click a link to confirm that they wanted to receive

Figure 5.20. A sample opt-in consent letter used by Bay Ferries, Great Lakes to generate opt-in consent from its database of prospects (*http://www.catfastferry.com*).

future e-mails from the organization or reply to the message to confirm their subscription.

It is important to make sure that you ask for the opt-in at every possible customer touch point. If someone is purchasing a product online, ask for the opt-in and integrate your e-mail marketing solution with your storefront so that your confirmation e-mails are sent right away asking users to confirm their subscription. If people are filling out a feedback form on your site, ask for the opt-in. If people are purchasing products at your retail outlet, ask for the opt-in. It's important that you get your information into your e-mail marketing program as quickly as possible to trigger the distribution of your confirmation e-mails. If you wait days, weeks, or months, you will see a low conversion of people who will actually opt in to your campaigns. Integrate everything with your e-mail marketing tools to ensure that you can maximize the growth of your campaigns.

Learn More About Your Customers

It's typical for companies to ask users for a few pieces of information before the users opt in, but some organizations get carried away with developing lengthy forms that actually discourage users from completing their online subscription process. But how can you learn more about your users if you don't ask them direct questions up-front? Consider the following options:

- Ask your newsletter subscribers to update their profiles within your e-mail marketing system. Their profile can contain different questions that you didn't ask them to complete the first time when they completed their profile. This is a clever way to get more-complete profiles on each of your clients. You may consider offering some sort of an incentive (e.g., contest entry, etc.) to actually encourage users to update their profiles in your system.

- Learn more about your users' interests by asking direct and indirect questions in each of the campaigns that you launch. Direct questions would take on more of a survey format in your promotions. Indirect questions mean learning about your customers based on how they interact with the content of your promotions. You can learn about each customer and profile him or her based on the interest expressed in the different types of content that you send them. For example, if each promotion highlights products A, B, and C and you send a promotion to 1,000 people and 200 click on product A consistently, you are safe to assume that these users are interested in product A. Through segmenting the database, you can then send this select group of 200 people a promotion geared only toward product A. This is a simplistic example; however, it illustrates how powerful such customer data can be.

- You always have a thank you page when users opt in to receive future promotions, right? Well, use this to your advantage by asking visitors directly on your thank you page if they would like to participate in a survey. This is a quick way to learn more about users right from the moment they start talking to your organization.

- You can ask users if they would like to participate in a survey directly from their confirmation e-mail. When a user clicks the confirm link to fulfill the double opt-in process, he or she should be taken to your Web site to view your subscription confirmation page. This page can contain a series of questions or a call to action to participate in an online survey. Always remember that you can learn from your customers even in the most simplistic scenarios.

6

Web Analytics—Learn from the Past, Change the Future

You had 50,000 unique visitors to your Web site this month? Up from 35,000 last month? Wow! That must have had quite an impact on your bottom line! Oh, you don't know...

Unfortunately, most companies that monitor their Web site traffic are in this very position, though at least they're doing something. Even more unfortunate is that many more companies don't give any attention to Web site analytics at all.

To make your online presence a valuable part of your business, you need to be paying attention to Web site analytics. In a 3G world, there is no other way around it.

How can you shape your future if you haven't learned anything from your past?

In this chapter we look at:

- Web analytics defined

- Common measurements of performance

- Monitor what matters to your business

- Determine what works—A/B testing as a start

- Go deeper—use it or lose it

- Bringing it all together—use what you've learned from other sources

- Segmenting your target market

- Choosing a Web analytics solution

- Closing comments on Web analytics.

It is not our goal in this chapter to tell you step by step how to roll out Web analytics in your organization; it would take far more than a chapter to do that. What we do want you to walk away with is a good understanding that this can help your business, and we want you to question how you can make it work for you. Everyone needs to start somewhere. This is where you should start.

Web Analytics Defined

Any time you're watching over what happens with an online marketing campaign or your Web site, you're technically partaking in Web analytics. The Web Analytics Association (*http://www.webanalyticsassociation.org/*) offers this concise definition:

> *Web Analytics is the objective tracking, collection, measurement, reporting and analysis of quantitative Internet data to optimize Web sites and Web marketing initiatives.*

Webopedia defines Web analytics (*http://www.webopedia.com/TERM/ W/Web_analytics.html*) as:

> *A generic term meaning the study of the impact of a Web site on its users. E-commerce companies often use Web analytics software to measure such concrete details as how many people visited their site, how many of those visitors were unique visitors, how they came to the site (i.e., if they followed a link to get to the site or came there directly), what keywords they searched with on the site's search engine, how long they stayed on a given page or on the entire site, what links they clicked on and when they left the site. Web analytic*

software can also be used to monitor whether or not a site's pages are working properly. With this information, Web site administrators can determine which areas of the site are popular and which areas of the site do not get traffic and can then use this data to streamline a site to create a better user experience.

Whatis.com posts the following definition of Web analytics (*http://searchcrm.techtarget.com/sDefinition/0,290660,sid11_gci933619,00.html*):

Web analytics is the process of analyzing the behavior of visitors to a Web site. The use of Web analytics is said to enable a business to attract more visitors, retain or attract new customers for goods or services, or to increase the dollar volume each customer spends.

Web analytics is often used as part of customer relationship management analytics (CRM analytics). The analysis can include determining the likelihood that a given customer will repurchase a product after having purchased it in the past, personalizing the site to customers who visit it repeatedly, monitoring the dollar volume of purchases made by individual customers or by specific groups of customers, observing the geographic regions from which the most and the least customers visit the site and purchase specific products, and predicting which products customers are most and least likely to buy in the future. The objective is to promote specific products to those customers most likely to buy them, and to determine which products a specific customer is most likely to purchase. This can help to improve the ratio of revenue to marketing costs.

In addition to these features, Web analytics may include tracking the click-through and drilldown behavior of customers within the Web site, determining the sites from which customers most often arrive, and communicating with browsers to track and analyze online behavior. The results of Web analytics are provided in the form of tables, charts, and graphs.

There you have it. Three different sources produce three different definitions. There is no one generally accepted definition of Web analytics, but the theme is the same across the board, and that encompasses all that is involved in measuring the success of your online activities.

When speaking of Web analytics, you will commonly speak of qualitative and quantitative research.

Qualitative Studies

Usability testing, interviews, surveys, and the ever-popular focus groups are all types of qualitative methods of measurement. Qualitative studies produce results that offer insight into the motivation and rationale of a customer for a given situation. Think of it as feedback or opinions, not facts justified by numbers. Qualitative studies speak more to the personal reaction of an individual.

Quantitative Studies

Quantitative studies produce results you can measure, such as the number of unique click-throughs to a Web page, the number of people in North America with broadband Internet access, and so on. The data here is objective and speaks more of the general population using structured research tools. Quantitative data is measurable.

When speaking of Web analytics, most of the time you're talking in terms of quantitative data—"this happened 2,000 times over 24 hours." Qualitative research is often used with quantitative research to help explain what happened by providing insight into an individual's motivation, attitude, and behavior. Together they provide very useful insight.

Key Performance Indicators

Key Performance Indicators (KPIs) is a common phrase in the business world and you will see it come up often when discussing Web analytics. Key Performance Indicators are also known as Key Success Factors.

A KPI is measurable and reflects the goals of a company. KPIs are used in everything from measuring the average time that customer service representatives spend on the phone with a customer to the graduation rate of a high school. When thinking in terms of Web analytics, your KPIs concern those measurements that make a difference to your business in relation to the Internet. In the next section we cover some of the more common measurements of performance.

Common Measurements of Performance

The first thing you need to do is establish what key performance indicators are important to your business model. What questions about your online customers do you want an answer to? Following are some of the more common measurements for you to evaluate.

Click-Through Rate

Your click-through rate pertains to how many people actual followed your online advertisement to your Web site or landing page out of the total number of advertising impressions delivered. This measurement is very basic and cannot tell you a whole lot except for an approximation of how much overall interest there is in a particular online marketing campaign you are running. Think of this as a general measure of popularity. This measure is general in scope because it could contain hits by search engine spiders, a single potential customer who makes multiple visits, and competitors that decide they want to exhaust your click-through budget.

Unique Visitors

"Unique visitors" pertains to how many individual people came to your Web site or landing page from a current marketing promotion over a specific period of time. This is a very basic measurement as well, but it offers a more accurate look at just who has taken an interest in your offer by filtering out double data and irrelevant visits. Make sure you remove the search engine spiders and crawlers from your statistics so that they are not mistaken as potential customers.

Time Spent

With your Web site you might want people to stay for a while—to have a "sticky" Web site. In contrast, your landing page's job is to get people through to the end objective as efficiently as possible. Monitor your statistics to see if that is the case. Is your target market able to reach their objective with ease, or are they getting hung up somewhere?

You can look at time spent per page or spent during an overall visit. If a lot of people are leaving within a matter of seconds of hitting your landing page, they are likely dissatisfied with what they see. On the other hand, if the target market is spending an inordinate amount of time on your landing page, they are likely confused, or having a good time, or maybe they got up to go to the kitchen to make lunch. Time is only an indicator. You need to monitor the click stream of your visitors.

Click Stream Analysis

What paths do the target market follow when they hit your Web site or landing page? Are they going right to the "buy" button, or are they getting distracted by a link to some other section on your Web site? Is the target market hitting a particular page and then leaving your site? Monitoring the behavior of your target market on your Web site enables you to refine the navigation and lay out a simple trail of bread crumbs to lead your customer down the intended path.

Single-Page Access

Look at the number of one-page visits to your Web site or landing page. This is where the visitor comes to your page but takes no action other than to leave. If that is happening on a frequent basis, you undoubtedly have a problem. It could be that your landing page is not effective at converting, that the page the customer hits does not show a direct relationship to the ad or link the target clicked on to reach you, or perhaps a shady competitor is trying to exhaust your ad campaign. Understand what percentage of your visitors are coming to your site and are immediately taking off. If you have a very low percentage of single-page accesses then you are fine; however, if you see a lot, that throws up an immediate red flag that you need to do some further research.

Total Sales, Leads Generated, or Desired Action Taken

Everyone wants to know how many sales or leads a particular advertising campaign generated over a specified period of time. This is also a very basic measurement. How many sales did your online marketing campaign generate? Maybe you have other objectives for your campaign—how many people signed up for that online demo or downloaded that white paper? If you are using your Web site to capture qualified leads, then how many leads did you get through your Web site during, say, the month of May? When tracking the number of leads generated through your landing page or Web site, you should also look at the number of those leads who become customers down the road.

Customer Conversion Ratio

Of all the potential customers, how many followed through on the action you wanted them to take? This differs from total sales because you are looking at the effectiveness of your ability to convert customers, not just a bulk number. Make sure you are looking at unique visitors so that you are not counting the person who came back 10 times as 10 different people. The higher your customer conversion ratio, the better. How many browsers do you have to convert to buyers to make a return on your investment? The average conversion rate for a Web site falls between 2 and 5 percent.

Cost per Customer or Customer Acquisition Cost

You need to look at how much your marketing campaign is costing you per customer to be able to determine your profitability. This entails taking your total marketing expenses (including all costs behind the campaign itself and the landing page or Web site) and comparing it against your new customer sales over the course of a single online marketing campaign.

If you are running a campaign and you are losing $100 on every customer you capture, then you need to rethink your campaign approach. As a quick note: the higher your customer conversion ratio, then on average the lower your customer acquisition cost will be. What does that tell you? Make improvements to increase your ability to convert browsers to customers.

Net Dollars per Visitor

This is simply a look at how much each visitor is worth to your business. How much money, on average, is each Web visitor worth to your bottom line?

Cost per Visitor

This information pertains to all visitors to your Web site or landing page, not just customers who make a purchase. It is important to understand how much each visitor to your Web site costs you so that you can work toward bringing that cost down to maximize profits. This information is also useful for forecasting and budgeting.

Average Order Size

This measurement boils down to the total dollar value of an average sale. When a customer buys, how much does he or she spend on average? Take this knowledge and think about ways to increase it and compare it to historical information over time to get a feel for what works best.

Does your target market just go with the immediate offer or do they take advantage of the add-ons to increase the average sale size? Monitoring this information over time can tell you if the average customer purchase is going up or down, and it can be used to watch the success of different product cross-promotions so see which generates the best over-sales size.

Items per Order

This measurement is closely related to average order size, but the focus here is on how many items your target market is purchasing with each order on average. Watch this number to see if it goes up or down over time. It is helpful for determining if your cross-selling techniques ("If you like this, we also recommend this...") are working.

Shopping Cart and Form Abandonment

The average shopping cart abandonment rate is around 40 percent. How many people gave up somewhere along the line in the payment process or on the second page of a three-page information request form? You have to know where the process fails in order to improve it. Do everything in your power to understand your market and make the intended objective as easy to accomplish as possible.

Recognize that a typical purchase process consists of more than one step. Do not just look at the number of people who gave up, but be sure to look at where they gave up so that you can pinpoint where the potential issue lies and fix it.

Perhaps your customer wants your product, but he or she does not want to create a permanent customer profile before completing the order. If that is the case, give your customer the option to buy the product without creating a permanent user account. On the other hand, maybe your lead got to the second page of your order form, saw another continue button, and got scared off because there was no end to the process in sight, so the customer decided it wasn't worth it and gave up. This can easily be rectified by offering the target market visual cues (e.g., "Step 1 of 2").

Impact on Offline Sales

Do not neglect the impact your online marketing campaigns have in the offline environment. Your landing page might be converting customers and you do not even know it, unless you are watching for it. How? Your Web site or landing page will likely include other methods of contact the target market can use to do business with your company.

This can be a difficult thing to track; however, you can make it manageable. You might consider setting up a phone number that is only available from your Web site, so that when a call comes through you know it is because of the phone number that rests on your landing page. Likewise, you can give customers the option to print an order form so that they can take it into your physical location where your staff can process the request. In both scenarios, you know the lead came from your online marketing efforts.

Return on Investment (ROI)

ROI is a measure of overall profitability. Take your profit from an activity, particular promotion, month, and so on, and then factor in the total capital you invested to accomplish your activity to figure out the ROI.

It came to my attention recently that nearly 75 percent of online advertisers don't monitor their ROI. They could be spending $60 to make $50. Boy, that seems like a great idea.

Ultimately the most relevant key performance indicators for your business depend entirely on what you are trying to accomplish with your online marketing initiatives.

Monitor What Matters to Your Business

What do you want people to do? That's a question you should be asking yourself. There are any number of things you can monitor, but I'm sure you have better things to do than overload yourself with data that doesn't really serve a useful purpose anyway.

Most of you reading this book will have a Web site that is e-commerce-oriented or is focused on generating leads. Measurements that matter to most of you will:

- Produce accurate and cost-effective information

- Be supported by and for company stakeholders

- Reflect and drive business results through positive change.

As an e-commerce Web site, you're going to be interested in critical data like the total sales conversions, how easy it is to go through your site's purchase process, and how well a promotion sold during a specific period of time. For example, how many of those 25 percent off gift baskets did we sell during the promotion week of December 3 to December 9? That's good stuff to know.

As a lead-generation Web site, you're going to be interested in critical data like the number of qualified leads that come through your Web site, what online tactics work best to generate leads, how many people signed up for your newsletter, or how many people requested your new white paper.

Other types of Web sites such as customer service sites and content sites are going to need to know other types of information. If your site is based on advertising, you'd better be able to tell your potential clients about the demographics on your site and what they can expect in return for their advertising dollars.

What you monitor will be unique to your business. For a brand-new company, your efforts might be on getting as many new acquisitions as possible, whereas a more established company might focus more of its efforts on customer retention. Monitor what matters.

Determine What Works—A/B Testing as a Start

If you're going to make Web analytics work for you, then testing is one thing you cannot live without. Direct marketers obsess over testing to see what changes generate the best responses. Why is it, then, that the typical online marketer does not measure and test its efforts? It is the most measurable medium out there!

A/B testing is a common approach to testing different creatives in order to make incremental improvements. Let's explore this a bit more here. You might want answers to questions like:

- Is short or long copy more effective?

- Is it better to use bulleted lists to emphasize key points as opposed to paragraphs of information?

- Does separating content with taglines or headers increase the number of responses?

- What happens if I bold or emphasize key points in the copy?

- What impact does changing the writing style, or tone, of your copy have on a page's ability to convert?

- What impact does changing the presentation of the offer itself have on results? "Buy one, get one free," "50% off," "1/2 price" showing the original $200 price tag with a strikethrough and the new price next to it emphasized in bold red font as $100, etc., are all different ways of presenting the same offer. Which method generates the best response from the target market?

- Does your offer perform better with vivid imagery, little imagery, or no imagery?

- What colors on the page elicit the most favorable responses? Does the contrast between the page copy and the background influence the response rate?

- What font types, styles, and sizes are most effective?

- How many navigation options work best? Am I providing the target market with too many navigation options such that they get distracted, or would the page be effective with more navigation options?

- Where is the best position on the page to place the "register" or "request information" button? When the target market completes the request form, the first thing you want them to do is submit their request, not cancel it. This means putting the "register" button as the obvious next step, before the clear or cancel option. Actually, don't put the clear or cancel option there at all—they're just distractions.

- Does the wording of the register or request information button generate more of a response if I play with the wording? For example, "Request a Free Vacation Guide Now!" versus "Submit."

- Have I tested different approaches for completing the action I want the target market to take? Does a short or long form work best? Does the same request form perform better if it is split across two steps on two different pages?

- Have I tested variations of my offer to see what generates better results? Maybe a free gift will help boost the response rate depending on what the principal offer is.

A/B testing helps you address answers to questions like those mentioned above. There is always something you can do a bit better to maximize your results based on your page goals and what you have determined as the basis

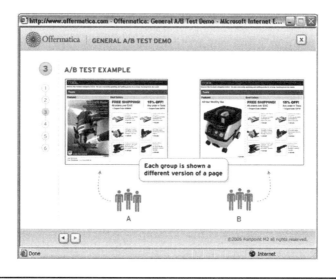

Figure 6.1. Example of A/B testing from Offermatica.

for measuring success. There are any number of tidbits you can test and tweak to refine your campaigns—some things will work, some things will not, but you obviously want to find out what does work the best and do more of it. Even the smallest changes can have a big impact. When running a marketing campaign, employ A/B testing to see which landing page techniques generate the best responses from your target market.

Here is a simplified way to think about A/B testing. Say you have an e-mail promotion you want to send out to your house list of 10,000 subscribers. What you're going to do is send 5,000 of those subscribers to one landing page and the other 5,000 subscribers to another landing page to learn which version is more effective. Figure 6.1 is an illustration of what was just explained. This example is from Offermatica, a hosted testing and optimization service provider.

When running a new campaign for the first time, it is difficult to say what will trigger the best response, so you might test two, three, or even five dramatically different e-mail campaigns, landing pages, PPC ads, or whatever it is you are testing. You would use the one that performs the best as your starting point for future refinements.

Keep It Simple

It is best to test one element at a time during refinements so that you can measure results and determine the effectiveness of the new change. If you change too many items at once, it will be difficult to attribute how much of an impact the items you changed had on the effectiveness of the page. If you made three adjustments to your landing page at once, it might be that two of the three components have increased the response rate, but the third might have dragged it down a bit, so you are not quite reaching your potential. If you change just one element at a time, you can tell what impact your change has on the landing page's ability to convert.

Give It Time

When running a test, you must let it run long enough to enable you to pull accurate results. You need to gather enough responses and give people enough time to respond to your campaigns. If you're curious about the immediate responses, you might look at some preliminary results a couple hours after your e-mail campaign launch, but a 1 percent sample is not really an accurate representation of the total campaign success. How much time you give a campaign ultimately depends on what you're testing; it could need days or even weeks to paint the complete picture.

Tracking Your Tests

There are many ways to make tracking your test results easier. If you want to test a couple of different offers, you might issue two different codes that the customer enters at the time of purchase. This makes it quite easy to determine the offer that was more appealing. Alternatively, you can use scripts or send people to different servers or different pages. As mentioned above, you might test two variations of a landing page to see which one more people respond to.

If A/B testing is something you would sooner not have any part in, there are companies out there that can help you run tests and conduct performance measurements. Optimost (*http://www.optimost.com/*) and Offermatica (*http://www.offermatica.com/*) are two reputable sources that can help you with A/B testing and other types of testing such as multivariate testing.

Web analytics will tell you how well you did, but you must conduct tests to cause change. One test alone will not give you all the answers. Using Web analytics and testing together to test, measure, and improve your results is an ongoing process. Capitalizing on any great campaign requires a great closing, so keep at it!

Go Deeper—Use It or Lose It

For e-commerce and lead-generation Web sites alike, knowing the conversion rate is a big deal. No doubt, knowing your site's conversion rate is hugely important, but here's the kicker. Knowing your conversion rate is like getting a grade on your high school report card. It will tell you how well you're doing, but not what happened between start to finish getting to that score. Did people get freaked out by the length of your contact form? Was the call to action not properly worded? Heck, did you go after the wrong people altogether?

When monitoring your results, analyze what happens at every stage of the process your potential customer engages in. If nine out of ten people are dropping out of your shopping cart at the same step in the process, you know something is clearly wrong and you can investigate it further.

Stay on top of everything and constantly watch your progress! You can make changes on the fly if a promotion is floundering to bring up your results. Say you run a promotion on your site and it is getting an extraordinary number of click-throughs through a certain call to action, but no one is taking you up on the offer. What you find particularly bizarre is that the link all along that has been converting is still there, but no one is clicking on it. What is happening here is link cannibalization. The former is drawing attention from the latter, but it is not speaking in the language your target market responds to—it's stealing the former link's thunder, but not producing any results of its own. If you are monitoring your results regularly, you can act on this immediately to turn it around.

When measuring your performance online with Web analytics, compare and contrast the information you gather with historical information. By looking at historical information, you can see the results of your current efforts against the past to identify trends and variations in the results. If you notice a new landing page has not performed as well as your previous landing page, then you know that little tweak you made did not benefit you and you can eliminate it from your next online marketing effort. If the little tweak you made to your landing page paid off, then you keep it and try something else to further improve your conversions and return on investment.

It helps to track the differences in behavior between first-time buyers and repeat customers. What motivates a first-time buyer in comparison to what motivates a return customer is different. With repeat customers, you have less convincing to do in most cases. You can use the knowledge you learn about new customers and repeat customers to tailor the experience to each market segment's needs.

Now, you've gone through all this effort to find out how you're doing, but in order for that knowledge to make a difference you have to be proactive and encourage positive change. Test different changes to watch their impact on your results. In the previous section we covered the topic of A/B testing and a variety of things you can test on your own. The whole purpose behind monitoring your performance is so that you can use what you've learned to change the future—you know, that whole "learn from your mistakes" saying. Don't lose sight of the big picture.

Bringing It All Together—Use What You've Learned From Other Sources

The more you know, the better when it comes to deciding what actions you are going to take to make updates to your online initiatives. You can use information from other sources with your Web analytics to paint a more complete picture of the situation at hand. Let's look at a few examples.

Industry Studies and Metrics

You see these all of the time. Companies like Forrester Research (*http://www.forrester.com/*), JupiterResearch (*http://www.jupiterresearch.com/*), nielson/netratings (*http://www.nielsen-netratings.com/*), and eMarketer (*http://www.emarketer.com/*) (Figure 6.2) frequently publish insight into online activities in many industries. Some of this research is free, and some you must pay for in order to acquire the full study.

Studies conducted by these market research companies provide great industry benchmarks that you can then use to sit back and say, "Okay, how is my business performing in comparison to the industry as a whole?"

Usability Studies

From reviewing your Web analytics, you know you have a problem somewhere, but you are unsure exactly what the problem is or what to do about it. Conducting a usability study will help you pinpoint the problem and tell you what to test to make improvements to customer acquisitions and retention rates.

In short, usability studies will usually:

1. Point out specific usability problems with your Web site interface in line with how well your Web site speaks to your audience and their goals

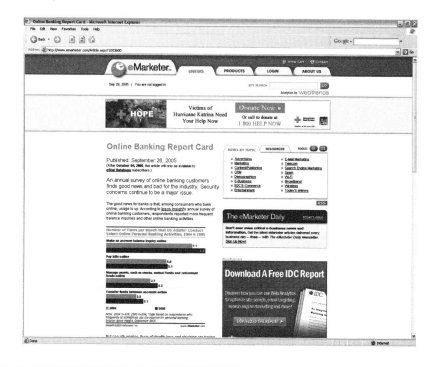

Figure 6.2. eMarketer is a great resource for industry statistics and studies.

2. Provide you with specific recommendations and direction on how to change your Web site interface to better adhere to the needs of your audience.

Usability studies are labor-intensive and require skills that are highly sought after, so you can expect to pay a solid price for a formal usability study—$20,000 and up is not unusual.

For more information on usability studies, we recommend you check out Jakob Nielsen's Web site at *http://www.useit.com/*. Jakob is a highly regarded usability expert.

In some cases existing usability reports are available for you to reference before you even get started on your Web site to get you off on the right foot. Are you looking at redesigning your e-commerce Web site? No problem; the Nielsen Norman Group (*http://www.nngroup.com/*) has a report with usability guidelines for e-commerce Web sites (Figure 6.3) that you can purchase for $129.

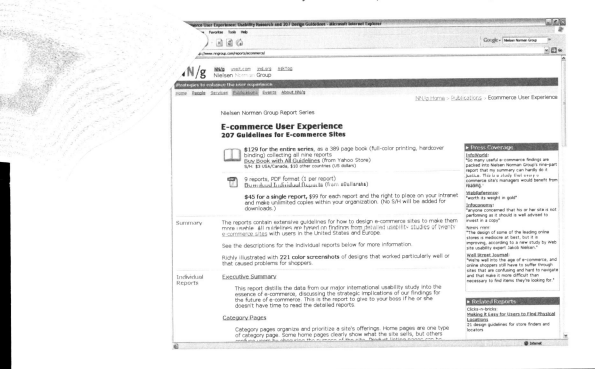

Figure 6.3. Nielson Norman Group has a report with guidelines on usability for e-commerce Web sites.

User Interface Engineering (*http://www.uie.com/*) is another highly regarded usability research and training organization.

Eyetracking Studies

Eyetracking studies can be considered a part of usability analysis. An eyetracking study allows you to look at your Web site through the eyes of your customer. If you are curious as to what your customers are drawn to on your Web site or are looking for ways to increase the productivity of your site, then one option to look at is heat maps. An eyetracking analysis produces heat maps that show you where a person's eyes are drawn by tracking eye movement on a page. In Figure 6.4 you can see where people are placing their attention. The red area is the priority, followed by yellow, and so on.

A company like Eye Tools (*http://www.eyetools.com/*) can provide you with eyetracking analysis services. The results of the studies then allow you

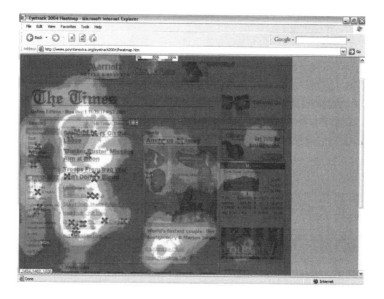

Figure 6.4. Heatmap example produced by an eyetracking analysis.

to better position, add, or remove items on your Web site that you want your customers to see and act on.

Competitive Studies

Any smart business knows it needs to be aware of what the competitors are up too. Make sure you do not neglect the online activities of your competitors and, instead, perform an online competitive analysis. Competing Web sites are often a great point of reference and will provide you with information that may not have crossed your mind. Look at what they are doing and figure out how you can do it better.

Customers, Partners, and Affiliates Studies

Ask the people you deal with on a daily basis for their input! Surveys, interviews, and focus groups can provide valuable input into the needs of your stakeholders. What does customer service have to say? Your staff who deal with customers for service-related issues are your front line to the needs

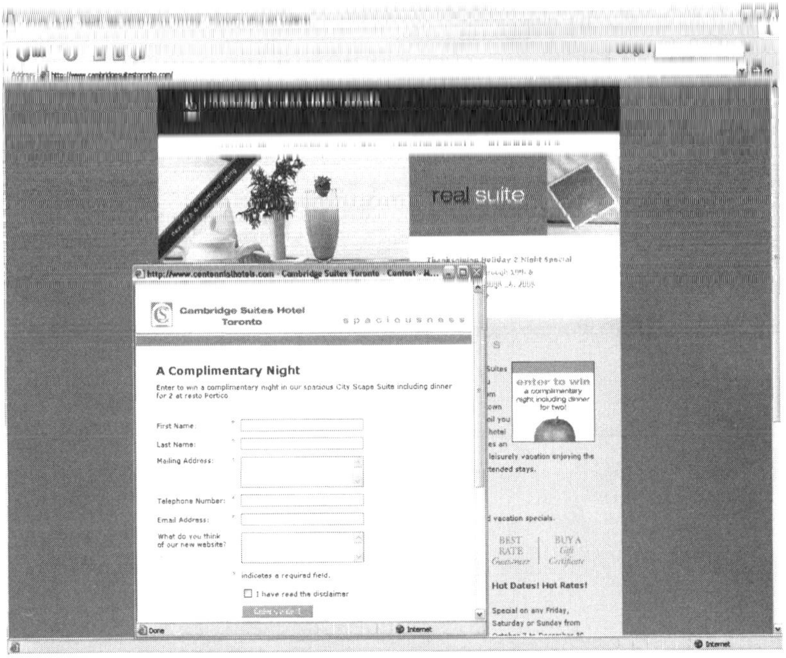

Figure 6.5. Cambridge Suites Hotel Toronto provides an incentive to collect feedback on its Web site.

of your customers. All of this information can provide valuable input into how to improve your business and adjust your Web site to meet market needs.

Surveys do not need to be complex! A client of ours, Cambridge Suites Hotel Toronto, is very proactive in soliciting feedback from its customers. When we launched their new Web site, we offered customers a contest-based incentive to provide feedback on the Web site to learn what they think of it and how we can make improvements. See Figure 6.5 for an example.

Your Web site can also be used to collect essential information on the performance of the business itself. Cambridge Suites Hotel Toronto (Figure 6.6) and the family of Centennial Hotels are customer-focused operations. Every time a guest stays with the family of hotels, the guest is asked to follow up with an online comment card after the stay. Immediately after the guest checks out, the customer is sent a thank you e-mail and an invite to fill out the comment card. The hotels use the information they collect to improve their services and to respond to questions from customers. This is a terrific strategy to build customer loyalty.

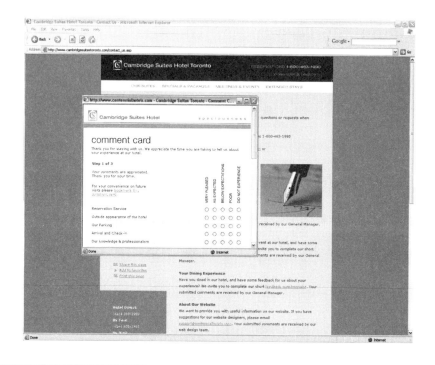

Figure 6.6.   Cambridge Suites Hotel Toronto's online guest comment card.

Ask your customers about their experience on your Web site as a part of the site itself or in a follow-up. You can employ surveys to ask customers a simple question about their experience on your Web site, landing page, or the offer itself. If your target market likes what you're doing, great; but if not, then follow up again to find out what you can do better. Most people will appreciate that you took the time to hear their concerns and know that you want to improve their experience in the future.

Site Performance Studies

Don't neglect the basics. Your Web site might be exactly what the customers need, but it takes 20 minutes to load so they simply can't be bothered. You must measure the performance of your Web site. Look at everything that could cause problems and potentially tarnish your image such as errors on the Web site, the speed of the server you're hosting with, the load time of your pages, and cross-browser compatibility.

You have to recognize that about half of the people with Internet access are still on dial-up connections, and many more simply do not have the option to switch to broadband for pricing reasons or simply because it is not available in their area. You also have to recognize that not everyone uses Windows and the latest version of Internet Explorer. What looks perfect in the new Internet Explorer might look like a garbled mess in its Mac OS counterpart.

There is a challenge in getting your offline and online data together, but you're not alone. Everyone struggles with this. Make use of other sources to try to close the gap on some of your unknowns.

Segmenting Your Target Market

Get to know who uses your site and why. The next leap in getting the most out of your online presence is to know how to speak to people and get them to respond. You know as well as we do that not everyone responds the same way when put in the same situation.

As an example, what we are asking you to do is to think beyond sending everyone on your e-mail list the same promotion. You will get more bang for your buck if you can segment your target market to appeal to specific interests and needs.

You will find that certain content is of interest to group A, but not to group B, and that group B responds very well to certain words that group A ignores, and so on. Confused? Think of it this way. Customer A's name is John and John has been your customer for years. John buys product from you month after month after month. Customer B's name is Jane. Jane has a need for your product, but has no idea who you are or how you stack up against the competition. Jane is at a different stage of the buying cycle and is going to react differently to a call to action that might work for John. John knows you offer what he wants and likes dealing with you, so he just wants to make his purchase. Jane, on the other hand, isn't so sure about you and wants information that will persuade her into becoming a first-time customer.

How does all this tie into Web analytics? You can monitor the behavior of your visitors and establish segments based on that. Very basic segments might include:

- People who are new or are repeat visitors

- People who are new or are repeat customers

- People who are customers or are seeking customer service

- People from marketing campaign X, Y, or Z

- People who subscribe to your newsletter

- People who are bargain hunters

- People who are quality-conscious shoppers

- People who arrived at your site from search engines, or e-mail, or through partner networks. (You would be surprised in the behavioral differences of people depending on how they find out about you.)

You really could go on and on, but again it depends on what you need to know. For your business, it might be important to segment your target market first by geographic region and then by another qualifier to get more specific. If you're doing business internationally, then no doubt you want to segment your target market based on geography, as how you speak to the general population in each area will vary based on different cultures, language, and preferences.

Figure out what particular segments mean to your business:

- What is the average order size of new and repeat customers?

- How much does it cost you to acquire a new customer?

- What is the market's affinity to be up-sold (e.g., new customers versus repeat customers)?

- What is the likelihood of repeat purchases? How often? How long between purchases?

- What do people like to buy online?

If you know certain repeat customers are likely to buy from you once a month, that they tend to purchase the same time every month as a refill, and that they have an affinity to purchase the items you "recommend," that is good information to know. Knowing this information, you can better predict the reactions of new customers as you attempt to convert them into repeat customers. You now know that a good frequency to send out an automated announcement is once a month from the date of the last purchase, that with the newsletter you might want to give people an option to receive a reminder notice refill their last order, and that you have a good chance of up-selling the market if you recommend trying a certain product.

Segmenting your target market allows you to get into targeted ads and customized content that appeal to the different characteristics of the segments. The more you adapt your message to your target market, the more likely they are to respond favorably.

Choosing a Web Analytics Solution

According to JupiterResearch (*http://www.jupiterresearch.com*), over $450 million was to be spent on Web analytics solutions worldwide in 2005. It is clear that the value of Web analytics is starting to get recognition. By using the Web analytics solution offered by Omniture (*http://www.omniture.com/*), automotive marketing services company Autobytel was able to increase its conversion rates by 18.5 percent!

Companies effectively using Web analytics know that marketing plans are just paperweights unless you can measure performance. They know that if they do not measure their performance, they increase their risks; and they know that by measuring performance, it helps them make informed business decisions that result in a better return on investment, more customer satisfaction, and in turn more customer loyalty. Another perk of Web analytics is that marketers are able to prove that their efforts actually do something—a great thing when trying to justify one's job or when asking executives for funding.

Look at Yourself

The very first thing you need to do is figure out what you're going to use the Web analytics package for. What are you going to measure and how does it relate to your business objectives? There are solutions that exist that offer far too little and solutions that offer far too much. There is no need to pay for what you will not use until you are ready for it, but be sure to choose a solution that will grow with you as your needs grow.

What reporting capabilities will you need and who will be using the package? If you need to be able to produce real-time reports, add it to your requirements. If different reports are needed for different departments such as marketing, make a note of that too. If you do a lot of historical comparisons, you will want to make sure you choose a solution that will let you compare data over time. Perhaps you want to be able to group visitors into specific segments. Assess the reporting needs of your organization.

What can you afford? There are open source solutions that will cost you nothing to more complex Web analytics packages that will cost tens of thousands of dollars. If you know what you need it for, you will be in a much better position to spend the right amount of money for your needs.

Look at Technology

Web analytic packages are typically ASP-based (hosted or on-demand) or stand-alones (software). ASP-based applications will use a snippet of code, such as a Java tag, to label every page of your Web site that must be measured. A stand-alone application is often a program you install on a local system to analyze log files.

WebTrends is a very popular Web analytics vendor that offers an on demand version as well as a software version of its popular analytics package. The following diagram (Figure 6.7) lists their own comparison of their on demand offering versus the software offering.

ON DEMAND SERVICE When you want all the power of WebTrends, with the speed and convenience of a hosted service. Learn More Try It Today	SOFTWARE When you want absolute control of your data and maximum flexibility to customize WebTrends. Learn More Try It Today
Minimal IT resources needed	Complete control of application in-house
No additional hardware required	Requires additional hardware
Pay-as-you-go monthly based on page views	Purchase licenses once + annual support plan
Uses only client-side page tags for data collection	Choice of client-side page tags or log files for data collection
Search engine spider reports not available (this is true of any hosted web analytics service)	Search engine spider reports available with use of log files
Custom reports available as add-ons	Unlimited custom reports without additional costs
Learn more about the unique benefits of WebTrends 7 On Demand	Learn more about the unique benefits of WebTrends 7 Software

Figure 6.7. WebTrends—on demand versus software.

What are your internal technology capabilities? Do you have the ability to install, run, and maintain an application in house?

Is the Web analytics solution compatible with your current Web site? Some Web analytics packages have trouble with dynamic content—content generated on the fly and usually with longer addresses that include database query strings. A dynamic address often will look something like: *http://stores.skipjack.com/dells/Search.bok?no.show.inprogress=1&sredir=1&category=swiss+maid+caramel+apples*. What about pop-up window content or content that spreads across different servers? You need to think about that, too. If you're running a storefront, then odds are the storefront is hosted external to your Web site.

Is the Web analytics solution compatible with your Web server? A package that can be installed on a UNIX box will not work on a Windows box.

Do you require integration with third-party software? For example, you might want to link the Web analytics package with your customer relationship management package. Think about the uniqueness of your business and its infrastructure to determine how you want a Web analytics package to fit into the picture.

Is the Web analytics package easy for you…

1. To set up—will they install it for you?

2. To maintain—are upgrades easy to handle?

3. To customize for a unique situation—a flexible solution is good to have.

4. To use—are the reports easy to generate and do they make sense?

If a solution is going to cause more headaches than benefits, you don't want it. There is something out there for every business, and it is just a matter of taking the time to find the solution that works best for you.

Many Web analytic packages offer evaluation copies for you to try out. Take advantage of it!

Look at the Vendor

Look beyond the technology and the functionality of the Web analytics package to look at the vendor.

Does the vendor keep on top of changes in Web analytics and how often are offerings upgraded or improved? This will give an indication of how current the vendor is and what is invested in research and development. You want to deal with a company whose focus is Web analytics, not 20 other things with Web analytics as a side dish.

What is the vendor's track record like?

1. Does it have a history of happy, loyal customers?

2. What are some of the results the vendor has helped companies achieve?

3. How long has the vendor been in operation and has there been a recent merger or acquisition?

Look at the stability of the company and customer satisfaction. You want to deal with a company that is well respected. ClickTracks makes no bones about promoting its recent awards—and well deserved at that (Figure 6.8).

1. What is the vendor's training and support like?

2. Do you have to pay for support? If so, what does it cost?

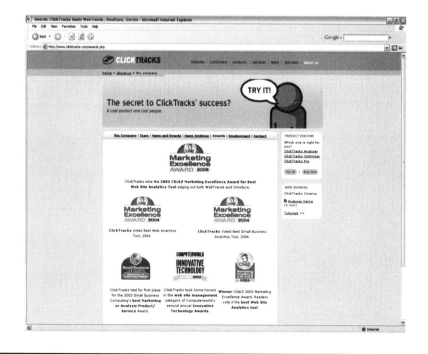

Figure 6.8. ClickTracks has won many reputable awards for its analytics packages.

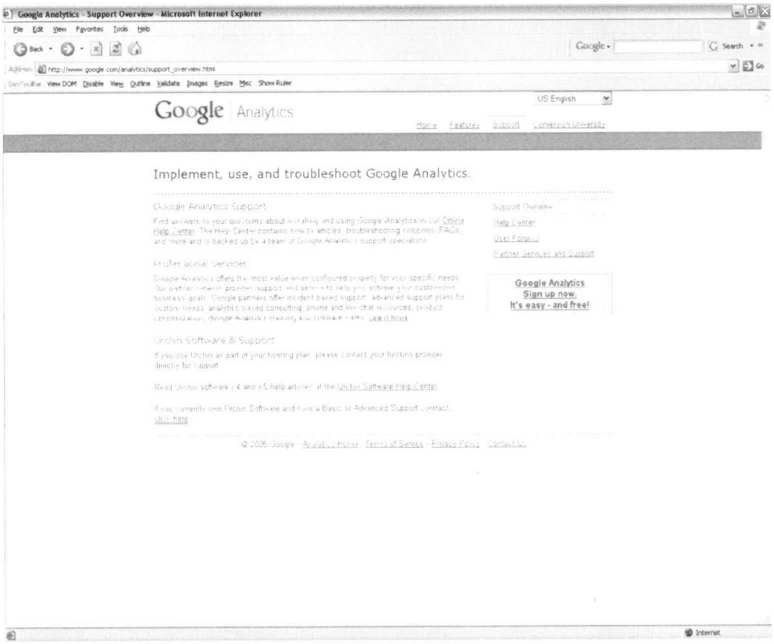

Figure 6.9.   Google Analytics has a support center for its customers on its Web site.

3. What are the support hours?

4. What support options are available? Examples include an online knowledge base, e-mail, and toll-free phone support.

4. What training does the vendor provider (online courses, manuals, etc.)? Does the training cost?

5. Does the vendor have community support? Packages that are widely adopted often will have a community of users that support each other to work out solutions. Odds are, if you're having an issue, someone else has already encountered and solved it. Take a look around for support groups and online communities. (See Figure 6.9 for an example.)

Popular Web Analytics Vendors

The following is a list of 10 recognized Web analytics vendors:

- WebSideStory (*http://www.websidestory.com/*)

- CoreMetrics (*http://www.coremetrics.com/*)

- Google Analytics (*http://www.google.com/analytics/*)

- Omniture (SiteCatalist) (*http://www.omniture.com/*)

- WebTrends (*http://www.webtrends.com/*)

- OneStat.com (*http://www.onestat.com/*)

- DeepMetrix (*http://www.deepmetrix.com/*)

- MyComputer.com (*http://www.mycomputer.com/*)

- IndexTools.com (*http://www.indextools.com/*)

- ClickTracks (*http://www.clicktracks.com/*).

All of the tools noted above are valuable to monitoring the success of your online initiatives. Each offers its own approach to Web analytics, so it is up to you to determine what analytics make sense for your business and marketing objectives and then select a tool that is compatible with your budget. For most businesses, a package from WebTrends, Google Analytics, or ClickTracks will meet your needs at an affordable price.

Closing Comments on Web Analytics

To measure the key performance indicators for your Web initiatives, you are going to rely on a number of assistive tools and old-fashioned analysis. Many e-mail marketing solution providers, pay-to-play search engine sites, and companies offering ad placement services offer detailed reports and self-service tools for monitoring your campaigns that can be used along with your Web analytics package to give you more information about your efforts than any other marketing medium.

There are statistics packages available that can track everything from click-throughs, your ROI, the lifetime value of a customer, the pay-off between organic and paid search engine marketing campaigns, whether your static ad or flash ad is performing better, and even the effectiveness of a link positioned at the top of a page versus one near the bottom. If you are running an online marketing campaign, then it is important to know if your efforts are justified.

In a 3G world, including Web analytics measures is a matter of good business. At the end of the day, remember that no marketing measurement is exact, but they provide you with insight on how well you are doing and guidance so that you can make positive change in the future. Strive to make your customers' lives better and you will reap the benefits.

Similar to the process behind developing the right Web site, you need to have a process in place for reviewing your Web analytics:

1. Figure out what needs to be measured.

2. Set up the appropriate systems and processes to track your key performance indicators.

3. Monitor your progress and results.

4. Review your results and make decisions about what needs to change.

5. Implement those changes.

6. Repeat the process to measure your results and fine-tune your performance.

Web analytics has come a long way in a very short time. You can just imagine where we will be a few years from now as technology continues to evolve. No doubt Web analytics packages will be become more advanced and easier to use.

We hope this chapter of the book has opened your eyes to Web analytics and its potential. We hope we have given you a lot to think about when you look into pursuing Web analytics for your business, and that we have given you enough knowledge to start asking some of the right questions.

7

Final Thoughts

By now you know how critical it is to take the time to plan your online marketing strategy, implement your campaign correctly, and make sure the appropriate tools are in place to enable you to measure the success of each of your campaigns. If there is anything we want you to take away from this book, it's the fact that you can't rush your online marketing plans if you want to succeed. Take the time to plan your strategy the right way.

We are going to leave you with these final tips, rules of thumb, and things to keep in mind when developing the online marketing strategy for your business.

Learn From the Success of Others

Staying on top of what the competition is up to plays a key role in the success of any business—both online and offline. It's critical that you watch what your competition is doing online at all times. Conducting a thorough competitive analysis isn't something that you do solely during the planning stages for your Web site. It's a process that should become a staple part of what you do on an ongoing basis. Mark off some time in your calendar to regularly review your competition's Web sites. What type of promotional techniques are they using? How are they keeping their brand in the eyes of their target market? Are they changing how they position their products in the marketplace? These are all things that you should constantly monitor in both an online and offline environment.

You should also make sure that you stay up to date on the latest industry news, case studies, industry reports, and white papers that are released on almost a daily basis. Reviewing case studies that highlight the successes and failures that other companies have had with implementing different online marketing campaigns is a great way to get insight as to how you can improve your campaign efforts and maximize conversions. It will also help you to identify pitfalls that you should avoid. Again, it just takes the time and the discipline to stay up on your research. Too often businesses treat this activity as mere homework that should come and go in cycles throughout the year. Make it a part of your daily or weekly routine!

Don't Be Scared to Fail

In the beginning, so many businesses were hesitant to take the first step and develop a Web presence. Eventually they were more or less forced to because, as we know, having a Web site became an essential component of any business's communication strategy. Now, we are seeing a trend in those businesses that are scared to actually take the next step and actively promote their business online. Remember when people were scared to shop online because they questioned the security of online shopping. This is the same thought process. They've heard the horror stories about companies' wasting money with online advertising, with implementing e-mail campaigns to get little to no return on their investment, etc.

It's those businesses that truly embrace what it is that the Internet has to offer that will succeed online. Those businesses understand that the Internet is going to play a key role in the future of business and are willing to take the time and invest the resources into the medium in an effort to succeed online. Embrace the medium. Experiment with different online communication channels and gauge the best avenues for you to reach your target market online. If your campaigns are not successful, don't let it discourage you—keep trying, and follow the proper planning procedures as outlined in this book to generate the exposure—and more importantly, the conversions that you're looking for.

Forget About the Hits

Remember, everything you're doing online is pointless unless you are objective-oriented. Sure, exposure is great and maybe that's the primary focus of your campaign, but even if it is, you need to set the tools in place to measure the true effectiveness of your campaign. At the end of the day, all the traffic in the world means nothing if you're not converting prospects to buyers. You could have millions of unique visitors each month, but what is the quality of those visitors? If you are not launching effective campaigns that are talking to your target market, you could be generating the wrong type of exposure. Without the proper data collection and measurement tools in place, you will not be able to determine if you're converting visitors or not. Think "foundation." Keep your objectives in mind; remember what you're promoting and always focus on your target market. The Internet provides you with one of the best communication mediums to channel specific target groups—take advantage of it.

Your Neighbor's Kid Can't Do It All

It's funny how many times prospective clients have approached us looking for Internet marketing advice and have made statements such as "my neighbor's kid can build me a site that will do what I want." Typically, these conversations result in a follow-up call six or eight months from the time of the original call as the prospect now understands that developing a winning Web site is much more than simply having an inexperienced developer throw something together and upload it to a server somewhere. As you know by now, there is a process to creating a Web site that will generate conversions, and it's critical that you follow a methodology of some sort to ensure that the foundation influences the entire process.

It is important to keep this in mind when you're evaluating potential suppliers to work with as well. For example, if you're issuing an RFP (Request for Proposals) to a sample group of Internet marketing firms that you are considering developing a strategic relationship with, make sure you don't base your decision solely on price. Evaluate their process and make sure that they understand that your Web site is not merely pages of code on a server. It's a customer touch point, and thus it has to meet the needs of your target market while enabling you to accomplish your online marketing and business objectives.

Don't be intimidated by the nasty "b" word. It's true that some companies are working with much smaller budgets than others, but the truth of the matter is that you can find a way to stretch your budget if you spend your dollars wisely and ensure that the process you're following when developing your Web site and implementing your campaigns is strategic. If you do it the right way, you'll see the conversions that you're looking for. Just take the time to do it right.

Often marketing departments face the internal struggle of warranting why their organizations should allocate a specific budget to online marketing. Typically they lose the battle because they cannot justify the reason they should do so. Statistics don't lie. In 2005, online ad spending in the United States alone will surpass $12.9 billion according to eMarketer. This is a sure sign that more and more companies are turning to the Web to help grow their business. Even more impressive is the fact that by 2009 companies will spend nearly $10 billion more on online advertising, reaching $22.3 billion.

Paint the picture to justify why your business should allocate funds to the online marketing budget. This is where the industry is headed. Support these statistics with case studies that prove that the Internet is helping other businesses—particularly the competition—to reach more customers, more quickly and in a more cost-effective manner. Trust us; once they see what the competition is doing and what they are missing out on, they will listen.

Take Your Time—Do It Right the First Time (or Second)

In the fast-paced marketing industry, everybody wants to complete things yesterday. It's a deadline-driven industry, and we've all grown accustomed to working fast to achieve objectives for our businesses. When it comes to your online marketing strategy and Web site plan, it's important to make sure that you follow the correct process to do it right the first time (or second, third, and so on). You don't want to invest time and money into something that is not going to provide you with an acceptable return on your investment. Sure, following a detailed methodology for building your Web site alone will take longer than simply sitting in a room on a Friday afternoon, laying out the structure and slapping together an interface for the site, but we all know what it takes to make a winning site. Think foundation. Think Q2C. Take your time and develop a strategy that works.

About the Authors

Susan Sweeney, CA, CSP

Renowned industry expert, consultant and speaker Susan Sweeney, CA, CSP tailors lively keynote speeches and full- and half-day seminars and workshops for companies, industries, and associations interested in improving their Internet presence and increasing their Web site traffic and sales. Susan is a partner of VERB Interactive Inc. *(www.verbinteractive.com)*, an international Internet marketing and consulting firm.

Susan holds both the Chartered Accountant and Certified Speaking Professional designations. She is an experienced Internet marketing professional with a background in computers, marketing, and the Internet. Susan is the author of several books on Internet marketing and e-business: *101 Ways To Promote Your Web Site, Internet Marketing for Your Tourism Business, Going for Gold, 101 Internet Businesses You Can Start from Home,* and *The e-Business Formula for Success*. She is also the developer of a 2-day intensive Internet Marketing Boot Camp. Susan offers many Web-based teleseminars, seminars on CD, and e-books related to Internet marketing.

Susan is a member of the Canadian Association of Professional Speakers, the National Speakers Association, and the International Federation for Professional Speakers.

As a result of technological change and global competitiveness, a strong Internet presence is essential. Susan instructs individuals with her enthusiastic personality combined with her vast hands-on international marketing experience, which keeps her listeners informed and captivated. Let Susan help you increase your traffic and make your business prosper!

Susan Sweeney, CA, CSP
SusanSweeney.com / VERB Interactive Inc.
Phone: 902/468-2578; Fax: 902/468-0380
www.susansweeney.com
www.verbinteractive.com
susan@susansweeney.com

Andy MacLellan

A natural-born leader, Andy MacLellan was raised in Halifax, Nova Scotia's capital city. A Commerce graduate from Dalhousie University, it came as no surprise when his strong ambition, entrepreneurial spirit and drive to generate results led Andy to becoming a partner of **VERB Interactive, Inc.** *(www.verbinteractive.com)*.

With many years of experience in competitive research, developing Web site architectures, and managing an extensive list of Internet marketing projects, Andy knew that VERB, an Internet marketing consulting and Web services firm specializing in delivering targeted solutions to travel and tourism industry clients around the globe, would allow him to achieve exactly what he'd set out to do. And that was to take action, transform challenges into opportunities, and create a never-ending stream of success and positive results. It was time to lead, not follow.

VERB's client list is a telltale sign that this firm has accomplished a great deal in the Internet marketing industry. Their ambition and passion for results promise not to cease. Andy has big dreams for VERB; in fact, he strives to make it the leading interactive marketing firm for tourism and hospitality operations.

Although sometimes accused of having a busy schedule, Andy still manages to travel and enjoy some leisure time. After all, there's no better way to know your target market, than to BE your target market. In his role as a "tourist," Andy can mostly be found fly-fishing in Northern Labrador or daydreaming about his next business venture while hiking in a remote location.

Clearly, hard work, compassion and dedication led him to where he is today. And hard work, compassion and dedication will lead him to where he wants to be tomorrow. VERB is about making sure your clients *know* what will get them the results they *crave* and *need*. Then, it's about taking *action* to make them happen.

Andy MacLellan
VERB Interactive Inc.
Phone: 902.444.7656;
Fax: 902.475.1847
andy@verbinteractive.com
www.verbinteractive.com

Edward Dorey

Halifax, Nova Scotia native Edward Dorey has never been one to settle for less than the best. He much rather prefers to continuously raise the bar for himself in the Internet marketing industry. What began in 1997 as a degree in commerce with a specialization in marketing from his hometown's Dalhousie University, has—nearly a decade later—evolved into a career that most young entrepreneurs only dream of.

Ed is a partner of **VERB Interactive, Inc.** *(www.verbinteractive.com)*, an Internet marketing consulting and Web services firm specializing in international travel and tourism. Clearly, VERB, the essence of action, was the perfect name for the company. To Ed, it symbolized being on the go; turning objectives into results; achieving; and moving forward and upwards, to the top.

By-lines on several industry-related articles and published pieces; contributions to a handful of e-books and published books; and even a published author himself, Ed's accomplishments and enthusiasm for the interactive marketing industry speak for themselves. What's more, he has years of experience conducting competitive research; designing Web site architectures; and developing targeted Internet marketing strategies for clients from Prince Edward Island to the United Kingdom. What clients don't know is that Ed's success has stemmed from his dedication to finding one-of-a-kind solutions for his clients; perfecting existing concepts and making sure his clients not only achieve their goals, but surpass them. He may not be a flamboyant, fly-by-the-seat-of-his-pants kind of guy, but his precise attention to detail ensures that everything is considered and nothing is overlooked.

Like most entrepreneurs, Ed can often be found wearing several hats around the office. But officially, his business card reads "Internet Marketing Consultant." He's obsessed with and devoted to transforming challenges into opportunities; helping his valued clients launch strategies to do business online; and ultimately leading them to results and success. Some people might call it "work." Ed? He calls it "fun."

Ed Dorey
VERB Interactive Inc.
Phone: 902.444.7656; Fax: 902.475.1847
ed@verbinteractive.com
www.verbinteractive.com

Appendix A: Global Online Populations

Nation	Population (CIA's World Factbook)	Internet Users (CIA's World Factbook)	Active Users (Nielsen// NetRatings)	ISPs (CIA's World Factbook)
Afghanistan	29.93 million	NA	NA	1
Albania	3.56 million	12,000	NA	10
Algeria	32.53 million	180,000	NA	2
Andorra	70,549	24,500	NA	1
Angola	11.19 million	60,000	NA	1
Anguilla	13,254	919	NA	16
Antigua and Barbuda	68,722	5,000	NA	16
Argentina	39.54 million	4.65 million	NA	33
Armenia	2.98 million	30,000	NA	9
Aruba	71,566	24,000	NA	NA
Australia	20.09 million	13.01 million	9.8 million	571
Austria	8.2 million	4.65 million	1.3 million	37
Azerbaijan	7.91 million	25,000	NA	2
The Bahamas	301,790	16,900	NA	19
Bahrain	688,345	140,200	NA	1
Bangladesh	144.32 million	150,000	NA	10
Barbados	279,254	6,000	NA	19
Belarus	10.30 million	422,000	NA	23
Belgium	10.36 million	4.87 million	1.6 million	61
Belize	279,457	18,000	NA	2
Benin	7.46 million	25,000	NA	4
Bhutan	2.23 million	2,500	NA	NA
Bolivia	8.86 million	78,000	NA	9
Bosnia and Herzegovian	4.03 million	45,000	NA	3
Botswana	1.64 million	33,000	NA	11
Brazil	186.11 million	22.32 million	11.63 million	50
Brunei	372,361	35,000	NA	2
Bulgaria	7.45 million	1.61 million	NA	200
Burkina Faso	13.93 million	25,000	NA	1
Burma	42.90 million	10,000	NA	1
Burundi	6.37 million	6,000	NA	1

Appendix A.1. Worldwide Internet Population 2004: 934 million (Computer Industry Almanac). *(continued on next page)*

Nation	Population (CIA's World Factbook)	Internet Users (CIA's World Factbook)	Active Users (Nielsen// NetRatings)	ISPs (CIA's World Factbook)
Cambodia	13.61 million	10,000	NA	2
Cameroon	16.38 million	45,000	NA	1
Canada	32.81 million	20.45 million	8.8 million	760
Cape Verde	418,226	12,000	NA	1
Cayman Islands	44,270	NA	NA	16
Central African Republic	3.80 million	2,000	NA	1
Chad	9.83 million	4,000	NA	1
Chile	15.98 million	5.04 million	NA	7
China	1.31 billion	99.80 million	NA	3
Colombia	42.96 million	1.87 million	NA	18
Comoros	671,247	2,500	NA	1
Congo, Democratic Republic of the	60.09 million	6,000	NA	1
Congo, Republic	3.04 million	500	NA	1
Cook Islands	21,008	NA	NA	3
Costa Rica	4.02 million	384,000	NA	3
Cote d'Ivoire	17.30 million	70,000	NA	5
Croatia	4.50 million	480,000	NA	9
Cuba	11.35 million	120,000	NA	5
Cyprus	780,133	150,000	NA	6
Czech Republic	10.24 million	3.53 million	NA	300
Denmark	5.43 million	3.72 million	NA	13
Djibouti	476,703	3,300	NA	1
Dominica	69,029	2,000	NA	16
Dominican Republic	8.96 million	186,000	NA	24
East Timor	1.04 million	NA	NA	NA
Ecuador	13.36 million	328,000	NA	31
Egypt	77.51 million	2.42 million	NA	50
El Salvador	6.70 million	40,000	NA	4
Equatorial Guinea	535,881	900	NA	1
Eritrea	4.56 million	10,000	NA	5
Estonia	1.33 million	620,000	NA	38
Ethiopia	73.05 million	20,000	NA	1
Faroe Islands	46,962	3,000	NA	2
Fiji	893,354	15,000	NA	2
Finland	5.22 million	3.27 million	NA	3
France	60.66 million	25.47 million	15.27 million	62
French Guiana	195,506	2,000	NA	2
French Polynesia	270,485	16,000	NA	2

Appendix A.1. Worldwide Internet Population 2004: 934 million (Computer Industry Almanac). *(continued from previous page)*

Nation	Population (CIA's World Factbook)	Internet Users (CIA's World Factbook)	Active Users (Nielsen// NetRatings)	ISPs (CIA's World Factbook)
Gabon	1.39 million	18,000	NA	1
The Gambia	1.59 million	5,000	NA	2
Georgia	4.68 million	25,000	NA	6
Germany	82.43 million	41.88 million	29.57 million	200
Ghana	21.03 million	200,000	NA	12
Gilbraltar	27,884	NA	NA	2
Greece	10.67 million	2.71 million	NA	27
Greenland	56,375	20,000	NA	1
Grenada	89,502	5,200	NA	14
Guadeloupe	448,713	4,000	NA	3
Guam	168,564	5,000	NA	20
Guatemala	14.66 million	200,000	NA	5
Guernsey	65,228	NA	NA	NA
Guinea	9.47 million	15,000	NA	4
Guinea-Bissau	1.4 million	4,000	NA	2
Guyana	765,283	95,000	NA	3
Haiti	8.12 million	30,000	NA	3
Honduras	6.98 million	40,000	NA	8
Hong Kong	6.90 million	4.58 million	2.60 million	17
Hungary	10.01 million	2.94 million	NA	16
Iceland	296,737	198,000	NA	20
India	1.08 billion	36.97 million	NA	43
Indonesia	241.97 million	12.86 million	NA	24
Iran	68.02 million	420,000	NA	8
Iraq	26.07 million	12,500	NA	1
Ireland	4.02 million	1.81 million	NA	22
Isle of Man	75,049	NA	NA	NA
Islas Malvinas (Falkland Islands)	2,967	NA	NA	2
Israel	6.28 million	3.13 million	976,000	21
Italy	58.10 million	25.53 million	16.23 million	93
Jamaica	2.73 million	100,000	NA	21
Japan	127.4 million	78.05 million	39.00 million	73
Jersey	90,812	NA	NA	NA
Jordan	5.76 million	212,000	NA	5
Kazakhstan	15.19 million	100,000	NA	10
Kenya	33.83 million	500,000	NA	65
Kiribati	103,092	1,000	NA	1
Kuwait	2.34 million	200,000	NA	3

Appendix A.1. Worldwide Internet Population 2004: 934 million (Computer Industry Almanac). *(continued from previous page)*

Nation	Population (CIA's World Factbook)	Internet Users (CIA's World Factbook)	Active Users (Nielsen// NetRatings)	ISPs (CIA's World Factbook)
Kyrgyzstan	5.15 million	51,600	NA	NA
Laos	6.22 million	10,000	NA	1
Latvia	2.29 million	455,000	NA	41
Lebanon	3.83 million	300,000	NA	22
Lesotho	1.87 million	5,000	NA	1
Liberia	3.48 million	500	NA	2
Libya	5.77 million	20,000	NA	1
Liechtenstein	33,717	NA	NA	NA
Lithuania	3.60 million	480,000	NA	32
Luxembourg	468,571	100,000	NA	8
Macau	449,198	101,000	NA	1
Macedonia	2.05 million	100,000	NA	6
Madagascar	18.04 million	35,000	NA	2
Malawi	12.16 million	35,000	NA	7
Malaysia	24 million	10.04 million	NA	7
Maldives	349,106	6,000	NA	1
Mali	12.29 million	30,000	NA	13
Malta	398,534	59,000	NA	6
Marshall Islands	59,071	900	NA	1
Martinique	432,900	5,000	NA	2
Mauritania	3.09 million	7,500	NA	5
Mauritius	1.23 million	158,000	NA	2
Mexico	106.20 million	13.88 million	NA	51
Micronesia	108,105	2,000	NA	1
Moldova	4.46 million	15,000	NA	2
Monaco	32,409	NA	NA	2
Mongolia	2.79 million	40,000	NA	5
Montserrat	9,341	NA	NA	17
Morocco	32.72 million	400,000	NA	8
Mozambique	19.41 million	22,500	NA	11
Namibia	2.03 million	45,000	NA	2
Nauru	13,048	NA	NA	1
Nepal	27.68 million	60,000	NA	6
The Netherlands	16.41 million	9.79 million	7.78 million	52
Netherlands Antilles	219,958	2,000	NA	6
New Caledonia	216,494	24,000	NA	1
New Zealand	4.04 million	2.34 million	NA	36
Nicaragua	5.47 million	20,000	NA	3
Niger	11.67 million	12,000	NA	1
Nigeria	128.77 million	100,000	NA	11

Appendix A.1.   Worldwide Internet Population 2004: 934 million (Computer Industry Almanac). *(continued from previous page)*

Nation	Population (CIA's World Factbook)	Internet Users (CIA's World Factbook)	Active Users (Nielsen// NetRatings)	ISPs (CIA's World Factbook)
Niue	2,166	NA	NA	1
Norfolk Island	1,828	NA	NA	2
North Korea	22.91 million	NA	NA	1
Northern Mariana Islar	80,362	NA	NA	1
Norway	4.59 million	3.03 million	NA	13
Oman	3 million	120,000	NA	1
Pakistan	162.42 million	1.2 million	NA	30
Palau	20,303	NA	NA	1
Panama	3.04 million	45,000	NA	6
Papua New Guinea	5.55 million	135,000	NA	3
Paraguay	6.35 million	20,000	NA	4
Peru	27.92 million	4.57 million	NA	10
Philippines	87.86 million	5.96 million	NA	33
Pitcairn Islands	46	NA	NA	NA
Poland	38.64 million	10.4 million	NA	19
Portugal	10.57 million	6.09 million	NA	16
Puerto Rico	3.92 million	600,000	NA	76
Qatar	863,051	75,000	NA	1
Reunion	776,948	10,000	NA	1
Romania	22.33 million	4.94 million	NA	38
Russia	143.42 million	21.23 million	NA	35
Rwanda	8.44 million	20,000	NA	2
St. Kitts and Nevis	38,958	2,000	NA	16
St. Lucia	166,312	3,000	NA	15
St. Vincent and the Grenadines	117,534	3,500	NA	15
Samoa	177,287	3,000	NA	2
San Marino	28,880	NA	NA	2
Sao Tome and Principe	187,410	9,000	NA	2
Saudi Arabia	26.42million	2.54 million	NA	42
Senegal	11.13 million	100,000	NA	1
Seychelles	81.188	9,000	NA	1
Sierra Leone	6.02 million	20,000	NA	1
Singapore	4.43 million	2.75 million	956,000	9
Slovakia	5.43 million	1.61 million	NA	6
Slovenia	2.01 million	930,000	NA	11
Solomon Islands	538,032	8,400	NA	1
Somalia	8.59 million	200	NA	3
South Africa	44.34 million	4.78 million	NA	150
South Korea	48.42 million	31.67 million	NA	11

Appendix A.1. Worldwide Internet Population 2004: 934 million (Computer Industry Almanac). *(continued from previous page)*

Nation	Population (CIA's World Factbook)	Internet Users (CIA's World Factbook)	Active Users (Nielsen// NetRatings)	ISPs (CIA's World Factbook)
Spain	40.34 million	13.44 million	9.84 million	56
Sri Lanka	20.06 million	121,500	NA	5
Sudan	40.19 million	56,000	NA	2
Suriname	438,144	14,500	NA	2
Svalbard	2,701	NA	NA	NA
Swaziland	1.17 million	14,000	NA	6
Sweden	9 million	6.12 million	4.70 million	29
Switzerland	7.49 million	4.60 million	3.50 million	44
Syria	18.45 million	60,000	NA	1
Taiwan	22.89 million	9.52 million	5.0 million	8
Tajikistan	7.16 million	5,000	NA	4
Tanzania	36.77 million	300,000	NA	6
Thailand	65.44 million	7.57 million	NA	15
Togo	5.68 million	50,000	NA	3
Tokelau	1,405	NA	NA	1
Tonga	112,422	1,000	NA	2
Trinidad and Tobago	1.09 million	120,000	NA	17
Tunisia	10.07 million	400,000	NA	1
Turkey	69.66 million	7.27 million	NA	50
Turkmenistan	4.95 million	2,000	NA	NA
Turks and Caicos	20.56	NA	NA	14
Tuvalu	11,636	NA	NA	1
Uganda	27.27 million	60,000	NA	2
Ukraine	47.43 million	5.2781 million	NA	260
United Arab Emirates	2.56 million	900,000	NA	1
United Kingdom	60.44 million	33.11 million	22.79 million	<400
United States	295.73 million	185.55 million	140.58 million	7,000
Uruguay	3.42 million	600,000	NA	14
Uzbekistan	26.85 million	100,000	NA	42
Vanuatu	205,754	3,000	NA	1
Venezuela	25.38 million	2.31 million	NA	16
Vietnam	83.54 million	400,000	NA	5
Virgin Islands	108,708	12,000	NA	50
Wallis and Futuna	16,025	NA	NA	1
Western Sahara	273,008	NA	NA	1
Yemen	20,73 million	17,000	NA	1
Zambia	11.26 million	25,000	NA	5
Zimbabwe	12.75 million	100,000	NA	6

Appendix A.1. Worldwide Internet Population 2004: 934 million (Computer Industry Almanac). *(continued from previous page)*

Index

24/7 business opportunities from Web site, 75, 79, 100
24/7 Media, 50
101 Ways to Promote Your Web Site (Sweeney), 34, 35, 91, 117

A
abandonment rate, shopping cart and form, 146
A/B testing, 148–151. *See also* Web analytics
  companies for performing, 151
  landing pages, 150, 151
  questions (samples) for, 148–149
  simplicity for, 150–151
  time for, 151
  tracking tests, 151
Accipiter, 50
action button on landing pages, 106
action taken totals, 144
Adrelevance (Nielsen/NetRatings), 43
AdSense (Google), 49
AdSonar, 49
"advertainment," 43
advertising center of Web site, 95, 96
advertising effectiveness from Web site, 75
advertising online, 41–51. *See also* banner advertising; search advertising; techniques for Internet marketing
  "advertainment," 43
  behavioral advertising, 49–50
  brand awareness from, 25–26, 43, 45, 48
  click-through rates, 42, 143
  contextual advertising, 47–49
  conversion of prospects to buyers, 49
  cookies and behavioral advertising, 49–50

"edutainment," 43
information search, Internet used for, 44
Internet industry overview, 10–12, 15–16
measurement and accountability, 45, 47, 49, 50–51, 91
placement of ads, 43
pop-ups, appropriate to market segment, 23, 48
rich media advertising, 42–43
size of ads, 43
skyscraper ads, 47, 48
targeting market from, 42, 44
AdWords (Google), 44, 45, 46, 100, 101, 115, 116, 120
affiliate marketing, 50–54. *See also* techniques for Internet marketing
  advantages of, 53
  Amazon.com, 51–52
  banner ads and, 52
  communication with affiliates, importance of, 53
  conversion of prospects to buyers, 53
  cost-per-action, 52
  "feeding" affiliates new material, 52
  fees, based on performance, 52
  issues of, 53
  landing pages and, 113
  link strategy and, 40, 53
  program management, 52
  quality vs. quantity affiliation, 52
  Really Simple Syndication (RSS) for, 55
  referral fees, 52
  targeting market from, 53
  technology evolving and, 53–54
  Web analytics for, 156–158
age differences of consumers, 5, 6
AlmondNet, 50

181

Reader Feedback Sheet

Your comments and suggestions are very important in shaping future publications. Please e-mail us at *moreinfo@maxpress.com* or photocopy this page, jot down your thoughts, and fax it to (850) 934-9981 or mail it to:

Maximum Press
Attn: Jim Hoskins
605 Silverthorn Road
Gulf Breeze, FL 32561

**IBM Software for
e-business on demand**
by Douglas Spencer
384 pages
$49.95
ISBN: 1-931644-17-9

**Building an On
Demand Computing
Environment with IBM**
by Jim Hoskins
152 pages
$39.95
ISBN: 1-931644-11-X

**IBM On Demand
Technology for the
Growing Business**
by Jim Hoskins
96 pages
$29.95
ISBN: 1-931644-32-2

**Exploring IBM Server
& Storage Technology,
Sixth Edition**
by Jim Hoskins
288 pages
$54.95
ISBN: 1-885068-28-4

**Building on Your
OS/400 Investment**
by Jim Hoskins
120 pages
$29.95
ISBN: 1-931644-09-8

**Building on Your AIX
Investment**
by Jim Hoskins
104 pages
$29.95
ISBN: 1-931644-08-X

**Conquering Information
Chaos in the Growing
Business**
by Jim Hoskins
68 pages
$29.95
ISBN: 1-931644-33-0

**Exploring IBM
@server pSeries,
Twelfth Edition**
by Jim Hoskins
and Robert Bluethman
352 pages
$54.95
ISBN: 1-931644-04-7

To purchase a Maximum Press book, visit your local bookstore
or call 1-800-989-6733 (US/Canada) or 1-850-934-4583 (International)
online ordering available at *www.maxpress.com*

Exploring IBM @server zSeries and S/390 Servers, Eighth Edition
by Jim Hoskins
and Bob Frank
464 pages
$59.95
ISBN: 1-885068-91-3

Exploring IBM @server xSeries, Twelfth Edition
by Jim Hoskins, Bill
Wilson, and Ray Winkel
208 pages
$49.95
ISBN: 1-885068-83-2

Marketing with E-mail, Third Edition
by Shannon Kinnard
352 pages
$29.95
ISBN: 1-885068-68-9

Marketing on the Internet, Seventh Edition
by Susan Sweeney, C.A.,
Andy MacLellen & Ed
Dorey
216 pages
$34.95
ISBN: 1-931644-37-3

Business-to-Business Internet Marketing, Fourth Edition
by Barry Silverstein
432 pages
$34.95
ISBN: 1-885068-72-7

101 Ways to Promote Your Web Site, Sixth Edition
by Susan Sweeney, C.A.
472 pages
$29.95
ISBN: 1-931644-46-2

101 Internet Businesses You Can Start From Home Second Edition
by Susan Sweeney, C.A.
508 pages
$29.95
ISBN: 1-931644-48-9

Internet Marketing for Less Than $500/Year, Second Edition
by Marcia Yudkin
352 pages
$29.95
ISBN: 1-885068-69-7